The Best
Women's Stage Monologues
of 2004

Smith and Kraus *Books for Actors*

MONOLOGUE AUDITION SERIES

The Best Men's / Women's Stage Monologues of 2003
The Best Men's / Women's Stage Monologues of 2002
The Best Men's / Women's Stage Monologues of 2001
The Best Men's / Women's Stage Monologues of 2000
The Best Men's / Women's Stage Monologues of 1999
The Best Men's / Women's Stage Monologues of 1998
The Best Men's / Women's Stage Monologues of 1997
The Best Men's / Women's Stage Monologues of 1996
The Best Men's / Women's Stage Monologues of 1995
The Best Men's / Women's Stage Monologues of 1994
The Best Men's / Women's Stage Monologues of 1993
The Best Men's / Women's Stage Monologues of 1992
The Best Men's / Women's Stage Monologues of 1991
The Best Men's / Women's Stage Monologues of 1990
One Hundred Men's / Women's Stage Monologues from the 1980s
2 Minutes and Under: Character Monologues for Actors Volumes I and II
Monologues from Contemporary Literature: Volume I
Monologues from Classic Plays 468 BC to 1960 AD
100 Great Monologues from the Renaissance Theatre
100 Great Monologues from the Neo-Classical Theatre
100 Great Monologues from the 19th Century Romantic and Realistic Theatres
The Ultimate Audition Series Volume I: 222 Monologues, 2 Minutes & Under
The Ultimate Audition Series Volume II: 222 Monologues, 2 Minutes & Under
     from Literature

YOUNG ACTOR MONOLOGUE SERIES

Cool Characters for Kids: 71 One-Minute Monologues
Great Scenes and Monologues for Children, Volumes I and II
Great Monologues for Young Actors, Volumes I and II
Short Scenes and Monologues for Middle School Actors
Multicultural Monologues for Young Actors
The Ultimate Audition Series for Middle School Actors Vol.I: 111 One-Minute
     Monologues
The Ultimate Audition Series for Teens Vol. I: 111 One-Minute Monologues
The Ultimate Audition Series for Teens Vol.II: 111 One-Minute Monologues
The Ultimate Audition Series for Teens Vol.III: 111 One-Minute Monologues
The Ultimate Audition Series for Teens Vol.IV: 111 One-Minute Monologues
The Ultimate Audition Series for Teens Vol.V: 111 One-Minute Monologues
     from Shakespeare
Wild and Wacky Characters for Kids: 60 One-Minute Monologues

If you require prepublication information about upcoming Smith and Kraus books, you may receive our semiannual catalogue, free of charge, by sending your name and address to *Smith and Kraus Catalogue, PO Box 127, Lyme, NH 03768. Or call us at (800) 895-4331; fax (603) 643-6431.*

The Best
Women's Stage Monologues
of 2004

edited by D. L. Lepidus

MONOLOGUE AUDITION SERIES

Published by Smith and Kraus, Inc.
177 Lyme Road, Hanover, NH 03755
www.SmithKraus.com

© 2004 by Smith and Kraus, Inc.
All rights reserved
Manufactured in the United States of America

First Edition: August 2004
10 9 8 7 6 5 4 3 2 1

Cover illustration by Lisa Goldfinger
Cover design by Julia Hill Gignoux

The Monologue Audition Series
ISSN 1067-134X
ISBN 1-57525-402-6

NOTE: These monologues are intended to be used for audition and class study; permission is not required to use the material for those purposes. However, if there is a paid performance of any of the monologues included in this book, please refer to the Rights and Permissions pages 100–104 to locate the source that can grant permission for public performance.

Contents

Foreword

This is the fourth year I have been putting together these monologue books for Smith and Kraus. Usually I have had a harder time finding monologues for women than for men; but this year there was, thankfully, a profusion of wonderful pieces for women, many of them *written* by women. I hereby dub 2003–2004 The Year of the Woman Playwright. Let's hope it's a trend that continues.

In this book you will find sixty-one terrific monologues. Most of them are for performers in their twenties to thirties; but there are several fine pieces for older performers as well. Almost all the pieces I have selected are from published and, hence, readily available plays. In the rare case of a monologue from a play that is not yet published, see the Rights and Permissions section in the back of this book for information as to how you can track down the complete script. Always try to read the whole play when you select a monologue to work on.

These monologues are culled from the best of the hundreds of plays I have seen or read in the past year. They are in a rich variety of styles. They are by some of the finest playwrights, both American and English, many of whom are household names (in households which care about the theater), but many are by writers whose names will be new to you, probably — playwrights such as Tom X. Chao, Tracey Scott Wilson, and Jordan Harrison, whose terrific plays are as worthy of your attention as those of Rebeck, Nigro, Baitz, and Blessing, included herein, the aforementioned household names.

I hope you will find herein the perfect piece for you; but if you can't quite find it, I strongly recommend that you check out other Smith and Kraus monologue books.

Break a leg.

— D. L. Lepidus

AMY'S WISH
Tom Sharkey

Comic
Irma, seventy-plus

> *Irma is an old lady who lives in a condo in Florida. She is something of a nosy busybody. Here she is talking to Sam, a retired newspaper reporter. She claims to be forty-six.*

IRMA: Guess how old I am! . . . Go ahead! You'll never get it. . . .
(Incensed.) Eighty?! (But quickly opts for a different attitude.) I see you're teasing me. I am forty-six. . . . It's hard to believe, sure — most take me for forty. And when I'm with my Barney — he's pushing triple figures, that's how we made the age cut — they think I'm even younger! Hey, when I drove us down from Jersey City — thirteen hours flat, including radar busts — Jeff, that cute little Jeff you met last night? — he tells me, "One of you *must* be over 55." Thought I was only *thirty*, he tells me later! — Course, it was pitch-dark out and he ain't seen my Barney yet, who's laying under the furniture in the back of the SUV. But Barney's lots more active now we're all moved in. Rain or shine he's out on our porch most every day, taking in everything — *everything* — you betcha. Saw *you* stumble up your stairs last night — *(Again looking about, perhaps for her real interest.)* but he couldn't quite see, uh, your pretty bride. Me? I spend most of *my* time down at the swimming pool where I have to fight off the, uh, more mobile of the gentlemen. *(Touches wig.)* Would you believe?, they call me "Copperhead" — like they're afraid I might slither up and bite them! *(Coquettishly confides:)* Which one day I just might! *(Feigning a yawn.)* But of course I'm home with Barney every night. *(Beat.)* So what the hell. *(Having checked inside the top of her sweater and found an empty pack of Camels, crushes it.)* Sport, you got a cigarette? It don't have to be non-filtered.

AT BREAK OF DAY
AT BREAK OF DAY
Noel Greig

Dramatic
Girl, twenties

The Girl is speaking at a press conference in a hotel.

The Girl listens to an unheard question and then answers.

GIRL: No. No, I don't think it meant my father did not love me. Well . . .
He was in a difficult position. And how was he to know that it was
my ear? Listen, it could have been anyone's ear. As I said, he was in
a difficult position — and the government has a very strict policy . . .
Yes, of course he must have known the risk, the danger to me . . .
Yes, I do still love him. Well, they didn't kill me, did they? . . . No,
I don't hate them. If you want to know, I think I was naïve and fool-
ish to go there, knowing the risks . . . No, I wouldn't call them fa-
natics, I wouldn't — will not — use that word . . . Of course, but terrible
things have happened there, things I'd no idea of, babies dying — no
food . . . Now? Well . . . Go home . . . No, not straight away, I want
to collect my thoughts — discover what my thoughts are. I'm not
sure what I've learned, maybe I'll discover that before I go home. Oh
yes, I'll tell you what kept me going. *(She produces the notebook and
reads.)*

> "Cowards die many times before their deaths;
> The valiant never taste death but once,
> Of all the wonders that I yet have heard,
> It seems to me the most strange that men should fear,
> Seeing that death, a necessary end,
> Will come when it will come."

Actually, that's what I think. Of course I can think someone else's
thought. Isn't that what we do all the time? Think other people's
thoughts and think they are our own?

BAD DATES
Theresa Rebeck

Comic
Haley, late thirties to early forties

> Bad Dates *is a hilarious one-woman play about a woman who's decided to re-enter the dating scene but who is having one bad experience after another. Done as direct address to the audience.*

HALEY: So I'm like, OK, this is just a date that's not going to work out. That's obvious and it's not the end of the world, frankly, I didn't actually think the first guy I went out with would be "the one for me" or anything like that, I was just trying to go on a date. So I'm OK with the fact that this is largely pretty damn stupid. And then, there's actually a point in the evening where having completely given up on this guy I sort of perversely got interested in his story. He starts talking about his ex-girlfriend. And the more he talks about her, the clearer it becomes that he's still, really, kind of in love with her. And the more I listen to him, the more I realize that this is more or less a first date for him, too, he's recently broken up with this woman he really loved, and now he's trying to get back on the horse. And this thought honestly makes me feel a little warmly toward him, I sense that we are fellow-travelers. And so I say to him, as a fellow-traveler, well, why did you break up? And he tells me this story about how — that your relationship with a person is like a movie. That when you're in a relationship, you see the movie, in your head, and that you need to see how the rest of the movie is going to go. And he realized that he couldn't see where the movie was going. He didn't know the end of the movie, with this woman. So he had to break up with her. And he looked so sad. Meanwhile, I'm listening to this, and trying to understand, so I say, What do you mean, a movie? And he goes through the whole thing again, about looking for the end of the movie, and your life with someone, and the relationship, and the end of the movie, so I say, you mean like death? Looking for the end of the movie, you're thinking about dying? And he says, No no no, it's not about death. It's about the End of the Movie. And we go around in circles like that for a while, and finally I say to him, I don't know, is it possible that you broke up with the woman you loved because of some insane metaphor?

And then he got mad at me. I don't blame him. I definitely was getting too personal. And I honestly had a moment when I thought, if you're siding with the guy's ex-girlfriend? It's not a good date. So then things were uncomfortable, and they kind of went from bad to worse, and by the end of the evening we were really annoyed with each other, and I let him stick his tongue in my mouth, anyway.

THE BUBBLY BLACK GIRL SHEDS HER CHAMELEON SKIN

Kirsten Childs

Comic
Viveca, twenties

> *This is a hilarious and very inventive musical, set in the early 1960s when black girls are getting blown up in Birmingham churches. Since it's so dangerous to be black, Viveca has decided to try to be as "white" as she can be. Here, she is auditioning for a "black" role in a play, and is trying as hard as she can to "act black."*

VIVECA: *(She says angrily:)* Hey, Director Bob! What do you think this is, camouflage? *(Getting control.)* OK — don't panic — black, black, black, black, black, black . . . lots of black people in the South . . . OK . . . southern accent, but not like a slave . . . 'cause if I do get this job, I don't want to offend the few black people that are gonna be in the audience any more than I have to . . . who has a southern accent? *(Thinks hard. Suddenly, an inspirational flash.)* Foghorn Leghorn! Ah say. Ah say. Ah say — Fawg Hone Lehg Hone! Yeah, that's good, but pitch it higher! *(High southern voice.)* Fawg Hone Lehg Hone! *(Snapping her fingers; in her own voice:)* That's *it!* I'm ready! . . . *(À la Foghorn Leghorn/Butterfly McQueen/Amos 'n Andy:)* Now Ah'm scramblin' — Ah say, Ah say, Ah say — Ah'm ska-*ram*-bull-in' up some eggs for buh-*reck*- fus', and here come — Ah say, Ah say, Ah say — here come mah boyfriend *Ros*-co, jes' a bu-*rak*-in' down mah kitchen doah. "Whu's wrong witcha, Ros-*co?*" Ah in — *kwhy* — *red*. "Wrong wit' *me?*" he says — *(Pointing accusingly, as if she is Rosco.)* "*You* da one — Ah say. Ah say. Ah say, *you* da one dass' been lyin' down wit' da *dawg*-ketch-*ah!*" Well, Ah neither cared for his tone of voice, nor his bad breff all up in mah face — hunh! So Ah picked up — Ah say, Ah say, Ah say — Ah picked up da iron skillet from off'n da stove and, *well* — uh — anybody — Ah say, Ah say, Ah say *anybody* care for some eggs and buh-*rains*-ah?! *(Winks again, then grins expectantly into the audience.)* How was that?

5

CATS CAN SEE THE DEVIL
Tom X. Chao

Seriocomic
N. Semble, midtwenties to early thirties

> *N. Semble is an enigmatic woman with an undeniably striking pres-*
> *ence. During the first two-thirds of the play, she sits at the edge of*
> *the stage and stonily observes the action except for a few brief in-*
> *teractions with the other characters. As the play unfolds, Tom (the*
> *Narrator) attempts to present a bizarre puppet show, which grinds*
> *to a halt after one of the three puppeteers performing the show rebels.*
> *Tom departs angrily and the puppeteers discuss things they would*
> *rather do on stage. Tom returns to lecture them about their acting*
> *careers. However, they refuse to continue the puppet show and leave.*
> *Eventually, Tom collapses on the floor after he begins to question his*
> *own sanity — he starts to think his thoughts are audible. At long*
> *last, N. Semble stands and speaks! She stands above Tom's uncon-*
> *scious form and explicates his deepest, innermost thoughts for the ben-*
> *efit of the audience.*

N. SEMBLE: Shh! Tom has gone to a strange place. At last, the wreckage of his failed puppet show has collapsed upon him, crushing his spirit. Or perhaps we should say that the puppet show has evaporated into thin air, since it never had enough *weight* or *substance* to collapse. *(She indicates the puppet stage, then turns her attention to the Narrator.)* Tom has gone to the place where he doesn't know if he's awake or asleep. He sometimes stays in this place for hours and hours. The only way he knows if he's asleep is when — *(An expectant pause.)* — he can no longer identify the origin of his thoughts. And then he knows he's dreaming. Yes, he's lying there with his brain cells chewing away on some meaningless problem — like the ending of his puppet show — and he suddenly finds that he's walking through a seedy, run-down German *Hofbrau* filled with arcade video games from 1981. But all of them are slight variants of readily identifiable games from that era. You know, the dream state where everything is unfamiliar except the *feeling. (Loudly whispering.) The feeling! (Pause. Normal again.)* But Tom has done very little, so his dreams are made of the cut-up bits of the few experiences he's had. He always dreams of being back in college. In his nocturnal wanderings, he drifts silently through endless white corridors in the halls of academia, or perhaps runs desperately between the stark brick buildings of the main campus, wondering, "Am I late for the lecture?" Or he finds himself in an impossibly tall dormitory teetering hundreds of stories over the Los Angeles skyline, sharing a crummy room with a stranger, thinking, "Haven't I done this before?" *(Pause.)* As he said, a long time ago Tom studied cinema at U.S.C.. He certainly didn't study theater! As you can tell. *(She smiles cruelly to underscore the harsh jab.)* And he worked in various departments on campus to earn money. Notably, he worked in the Psychology Department as an administrative assistant, though he was quite inefficient and careless and, well, useless. *(Pause.)* And today he still dreams of those days. Worst of all is when Tom dreams of suddenly realizing he's missed half a semester of Ph.D. classes and he'll never get a doctorate and his life is more than half over and he's going to *die alone.* He's probably going to die alone in this very theater. *(She indicates the theater.)* After hours of this suspension between states, he staggers to his feet and wonders if he's been asleep or awake. *(Pause. She considers him further.)* Now he's being purged in the great fire of madness. *(Smiles.)* He thinks people can hear his thoughts! *(Coyly.)* Do you think he'll be reborn anew after passing through the excoriating pain of insanity? *(Pause.)* Most people can't survive it. *(Pause.)* Do you know what can free him from his madness? Tom believes that only one thing can do that — do you know what it is? *(Pause.)* He believes a woman's kiss can save him! *(She laughs, lightly and musically.)* All lonely wankers believe a woman's kiss can save them! *(She moves to the Narrator, bends down, leans over, caresses his head, then kisses him.)* How wrong they are! A woman's kiss is a great reward, given in return for a man's service and obedience. It's not an IV drip bag full of life-giving fluids to be administered in emergencies! *(Seriously.)* Nothing will save Tom.

CATS CAN SEE THE DEVIL
Tom X. Chao

Comic
Tuesday, early twenties

> *Tuesday is a young actress who recently graduated from drama school Here, she speaks of her dreams and goals to Adrienne, a fellow struggling actress. Tuesday moves to center stage, still clutching her head shot.*

TUESDAY: *(Dreamily.)* I wish I was famous. Wouldn't that be nice? I wish I didn't have to perform in tiny theaters that nobody's ever heard of. I wish I could play the lead role in a big show on Broadway. With my name up in lights. I wish I could appear on TV and in movies and in magazines. And everyone would know who I was. I'd be so famous, people everywhere would recognize me. Everywhere, all over the world. *(Gradually more dramatic.)* I wish I was so famous that even people in the most remote locations on earth would be familiar with me. Even in the most hellish, disease-ridden, war-stricken, famine-ravaged, politically unstable countries, people would all know me! Though they have no food to eat or water to drink, they could draw spiritual and emotional sustenance from the image of my face! My face! Shining down from billboards and TVs and magazine covers! Bringing life to the arid desert and frozen tundra! My face! . . .

Well, you've got to have a dream. *(Pause.)* Oh, I know it sounds egotistical. But you'd like to think that you could rise above the level of — *(She looks around, shrugs.)* You know.

THE COMING WORLD
Christopher Shinn

Dramatic
Dora, twenties to thirties

Dora is talking to Ty about the night her ex-boyfriend Ed, Ty's brother, died.

DORA: That fucking night. After you left. It was horrible. Eddie kept drinking, right. Then this guy Martin showed up, like three hours later
than he was supposed to. Do you know this guy? . . .

Martin. Works at the casino, he's a bartender, and Eddie —
thought he might help him get a job there, right? So we're talking and
drinking and Eddie keeps, like, bringing up jobs and stuff, but Martin's not — he's not saying anything about jobs, right? Then Martin
kinda leans in and says, "Wanna know a secret?" And Eddie's like,
"Sure." And Martin says, "You know why you get so many free drinks
in a casino?" And Eddie's like, "Because the drunker you are, the more
you'll gamble." And Martin gets all quiet, like he's being all bad by telling
us this, and says, "No." He says, "We want, we give out free drinks because we want you to feel like everyone here is your friend." *(Pause.)*
"We do it so you'll associate the casino with getting something for free,
with generosity. That's what makes you gamble more. We actually don't
want you drunk, we actually pump oxygen into the casino to keep you
sober and awake." And Martin *laughs.* I think it's gross, this guy, talking about how they trick people into losing their money, but I look at
Eddie — and Eddie's got this look on his face like — he's entranced.
Like this is the coolest thing. But Eddie — I'm thinking, like — Eddie
works hard. All his jobs, you can't fuck anyone over in those jobs, they
can just fuck you. Eddie moves boxes. Eddie drives trucks, mows lawns,
plows snow. Eddie gets fucked over all the time, so — why does he
think this is all cool? Anyway, the night goes on — Martin doesn't say
a *word* about any job. Takes out a bag of coke, Eddie's eyes go real big,
like — that was it. Dragged him out of there, drove him home, puking in my car, put him in bed, and left. *(Pause.)* And . . . that was the
last time I saw him. That night. Blacked out, puking all over himself.
Called him the next day and dumped him.

THE DEATH OF FRANK
Stephen Belber

Dramatic
Natalie, twenties

> *In this direct address to the audience, Natalie is talking about her complicated relationship with her brother Peter.*

NATALIE: *(To audience.)* My brother will try to understand me for a stupidly long amount of time. On the day that I reach puberty he will knock on my door and request automatic entry. The reasons for my denying him access to my inner chamber will be because I did not choose him. I will want to choose the person to whom I acquiesce. This is why I will need Frank. For there is a part of me which always wants to give in, the part which occasionally *insists* on being on the bottom. It isn't a female thing, because I feel quite strongly that men have it too. No one wants to be on top forever . . . except for people like Frank. Frank will always be an "on top" guy. He'll work very hard to remain on top without hurting me. In fact, that will be *his* way of being on the bottom; he'll attempt to be on top . . . *gently.* He won't slam me, he'll ride. He won't thrust, he'll query. That's really what it is. Frank will query me with his love even though his instinct will be to shove it inside of me as hard as he can. And I will respect that. Peter is different. He will always love me the wrong way, wanting to know me in a way that a brother shouldn't know his sister. He will, throughout the course of my life, be consumed by me in a way that seeks not to shove his love deep inside me, but rather, to attach it to the top of a pipe cleaner and quietly, but without asking, probe the inner workings of my heart.

THE DEATH OF FRANK
Stephen Belber

Dramatic
Lynn, twenties to thirties

Lynn, a linguist, is addressing an unseen audience.

LYNN: . . . The N.R.A., for example, is a paranoid, fundamentalist-backed organization full of tight-buttocked men who don't know the difference between a prostate and a prostitute; be that as it may, I still believe in guns. In fact, I carry one with me twenty-four/seven — *(She produces a very large pistol and brandishes it for the next several sentences.)* — not because I plan to shoot anyone, but simply because of its superior deterrent quality; negotiation leverage. It helps me to ar-ti-cul-late. Why? — well, call me an old-fashioned pork bun who doesn't know her mouth from her anus, but I believe in words, Bob's your uncle, Fanny's your aunt, spank a semantic and call me in the morning — *(Calling offstage.)* How're we doing on time, Johnny? — good — *(Back out.)* — The point is, the relationships which human beings form with one another are rigid, immutable structures. We love who we love, we hate who we hate and there's not a damn thing to be done about it. We *try* — we kill each other a thousand times a day but it doesn't change the *facts.* Our only option, then, is to talk. *(She holds up a sign that reads: Communi-fucking-cation.)* It's a Greek word. But the problem with human beings is — we *don't* talk. We succumb to its seductive antithesis, which is violence. For violence is the key that unlocks the human heart. *It* speaks to *us.* What does it say? — It says, "Love me, darling, love me!" Am I being clear? — am I semiotically sparking your sagebrush? Violence is that chatty next-door neighbor who incessantly borrows butter until the day she cuts your throat. *We must learn to lock our door.* If we succeed, the world will work. If we don't, then we will all die violently at the hands of our partners. These are the facts — deal with them. I love you all. Thank you.

DEBT
Seth Kramer

Dramatic
Molly, twenties to thirties. A knockout.

> *Molly is an amoral man-eater. She spends the night with the only man she has ever loved and here pleads with him to stay.*

MOLLY: I don't pretend to know everything about men. Not all of them. Just a few. A certain kind of man. I know him after five minutes in a room together. That restless thing. That wandering eye. I know him, right there, as soon as he looks at me. A little work, a little interest, a little contact and I know exactly what comes next.

(Beat.)

It's power knowing you can take someone away from whatever life they're living. Knowing even more that they want that. Want you to take them.

(Pause.)

When she's right there. When she's in the same room. Sometimes it's worth doing just for the look on her face. Five minutes for me and three hours for them. Fighting about it later. It's power.

(Pause.)

I can find that type every time I walk out the door but you . . . I've never found anyone who can make me feel like you do. You're like a drug for me. A feeling that . . . I can't even describe it . . . when I'm fucking them, when I feel them under my body . . . I think of you. You're the voice I hear when they say my name.

(Pause.)

Today, when I walked in and saw you standing in the living room, I almost — almost . . .

(Beat.)

I thought I was dreaming — that you couldn't be real. My legs actually shook. So many times — for months after you left — I'd come home hoping to find some trace of you — a sign you'd come back — your coat hanging in the closet, your keys on the table. Anything. I waited and waited hoping, worrying, doubting myself . . .

(Beat.)

And now here you are.

(Beat.)

I'm glad you came back, baby. It's been so long. I started to think . . . think I'd lost you . . . That you'd found someone else. I couldn't deal with that.

(Beat.)

You should stay here tonight. It's just been so long . . . The way you know me. My body. We can take a shower together. Whatever you want. Alright?

(Pause.)

I'll help you get the money. Everything will be fine now. Now that you're back.

(Pause.)

I know I can help you.

FEED THE HOLE
Michael Stock

Dramatic
Shelly, twenties

Shelly is telling off her boyfriend, Brett.

SHELLY: No more! I'm too tired. I'm over it! Over my life! Over my friends. Their faults annoy the shit out of me. And I'm over you! Your touch's mean. And I can't have you inside me like that. I need to go and sleep now. Never again on the closet floor. Sleep. In a bed that's safe. Sleep. And not wake up. Because I keep working and working on your happiness. But you aren't ready to be happy. I'm going to Samantha and Rob's. Don't call me. I'm going to sleep, and plant rocks. Because I really — I need to feed this hole in my chest that's killing me. And I pray to God — No not God! Fuck God! God gives me no relief! I pray and no one answers! — I hope, I hope you feed that hole. Because I loved you once. But your foundation's all fucked up, and your house's going to sink. And I can't wait on my side of the bed until it's sunk, and you're in a midlife crisis because we haven't touched for years, and you're always working or on the couch eating that dulce de leche ice cream, and our life and me are not what you want, so you're leaving for some young, thin, dumb Barbie blond. And I get up and look in the mirror, not the fun-house mirror I've been staring in all these years, where my sideshow insecurities are so distorted so I'm only sad eyes and big hips, but a real reflection, where I see what the hell have I done?!; I'm not your fucking maid! Pick up your clothes to show you care about me. I mop and mop, but I can't scrub this place clean. It's filled with hurt and failure. And — I've burnt all the pots, Brett. I want a family and kids and someone who looks at me like that, with that knowing, smiling, burning, yearning desire, and I want the type of security I feel secure in and I really — This is not at all what I planned to say. I didn't want to say all that stuff. But I'm so hurt and my mouth keeps going and I can't, for the life of me, figure out how to shut up and walk out that door. And I'm sorry. I'm sorry I hurt you. I'm sorry I can't be whatever you need. But I can't figure out what that is. I can't. I'm too hurt. I'm too tired. And now — and now — I'm going to turn around and walk out that door. And I would really appreciate it — it would really mean a lot to me if you didn't say anything till I'm gone, because I don't think I can handle any more of this conversation, and I'm not prepared to start bawling. 'Cause I don't think I'll stop. Ever.

FIGHTING WORDS
Sunil Kuruvilla

Dramatic
Peg, twenty-five

> *Peg is a Welsh woman in love with boxing and in love with local*
> *hero, boxer Johnny Owen, who's fighting a bout in Los Angeles for*
> *the world welterweight title. Here she is talking to her sister, Nia,*
> *about why she and Johnny are, as they say, made for each other.*

PEG: I know Johnny's hands. *(Silence. Peg slowly starts to confess her rela-*
tionship with Johnny to her sister.) Every Saturday night, Johnny and
I meet in the basement of the church with the rest of you. We wait
until everyone starts dancing close then we sneak away. We go to the
gym. I boost Johnny to the window. I can't fit through but he can.
He comes around and unlocks the door. You don't want to hear the
rest. . . .

Johnny never likes to take his shirt off. I have to go first. My
skirt. His trousers. My stockings. His socks. Stripped naked, we dress
each other. Working from the ground up. Socks, shoes. Leather cup.
The laces rub my spine. Satin trunks tied in the front. The knot
against my belly. Fingers on my lips. His rough hands rub Vaseline
on my face. . . .

We try to make each other bleed. Eyes wide open. Seeing everything. I'm bigger but he's quicker. I try to get inside on him, close
the distance. I make him go hard: *(Shouts:)* "Don't hold back! Floor
me! Go for my body!" *(Peg moves toward Nia.)* Hook to the kidney.
Shot to the belly. He makes me ache. But I study his body. He drops
his shoulder after double jabbing. He sits down on his back foot. He
always backs away shocked when I figure him out. In the end we come
together. A tired clinch. *(Peg clinches Nia.)* Shoulder to shoulder. Our
arms hooked together to keep the other from punching. Breathing
each other's breath. Exhausted. Alive. You hear your man breathe. You
hear yourself.

FIVE FLIGHTS
Adam Bock

Dramatic
Olivia, thirties

> *Olivia is a driven woman who believes that she has received a call-*
> *ing from God to build a church with a most unusual theology.*

OLIVIA: OK.

One day, when I was practicing preaching, outside, it rained. I thought "We're gonna need a church. With a roof." And a miracle happened. Because that very day, Adele said to me — "My father is dead." *(Long pause.)*

Now.

In order to understand why I knew this was a miracle, we have to go back in time.

Imagine:

Two years ago, on the fifth day of my semiannual fast, which also happened to be on Cinqo de Mayo, the fifth of May, which is the fifth month of the year, I was wandering through the basement stacks of the Rochambeau library. Just I was light-headed. Well because I was fasting. I was light-headed. I was discouraged. I had a low-paying job.

My car was. My Visa bill was. I felt.

I was in the basement of a library.

So there I was. In the basement. Just reading. Here and there. And I opened a journal. With an article. About a medieval aviary. Not a building aviary. But a book aviary. A medieval book. Written by monks. Which explained everything. In the form of stories about birds.

The vulture devours corpses like a sinner delights in carnal knowl-edge. And. The sparrow is an inconstant and restless bird. Like a faith-less man flying from God. And . . .

Right. And. Suddenly a flashing insight cut through my light-headedness and despair.

I realized the bird is God revealing all. On the fifth day of the fifth month of my fortieth year and forty is five times five plus five and five and five, I realized that the fifth day of creation is really the holiest of holy days. Not the sixth, not the seventh, but the fifth. The day God created birds.

And I felt a deep calm. I had a message to share.

I went to work. With the number five and flocks of birds flying around in my head. I went to my low-paying job but so what I don't care. I was working at the paint department at Adler's. So what.

FIVE FLIGHTS
Adam Bock

Dramatic
Jane, thirties to forties

> *Jane is furious that her siblings appear ready to turn over her late*
> *father's aviary to Olivia, who plans to use it as a church based on*
> *a theology having to do with birds.*

JANE: It's a peewee. . . . But to Olivia it's a symbol. It's a call to action. Action that will lead to asphalt and an aviary cathedral, and to the formation of a doctrine, and of course doctrine leads to a lack of imagination and a lack of imagination leads to a feeling of scarcity because we can't imagine the world any other way, all we can hope for is the small world we already see, and as a result all we feel is scarcity and then of course we have the urge to purchase things, to try and fill ourselves up, so what this bird as symbol leads us to is a feeling of overwhelming scarcity, to the feeling of scarcity that is the basic fuel of consumerism.

That's the problem with symbolism. It presents us with answers. It stops us from thinking. That's the problem with doctrine. It stops us from thinking. That's the problem with telling others what to think. It stops them from thinking. That's my problem with Olivia. It's maddening! . . .

It is. It's maddening! It's infuriating! . . .

She'll continue to spout this bird nonsense and the faithful will tromp after her, faithfully flattening everything in their way! Who's going to clean up after her spiritual mess? She's like those movie supercops crashing cars and blowing up buses in order to catch the criminal! Who sweeps up the glass? Who cleans up?

FISHER KING

Don Nigro

Dramatic
Mrs. Walsh, thirty-four

Mrs. Welsh sits alone on her porch in the woods in a remote cabin somewhere near where Maryland, Virginia, West Virginia, and Pennsylvania come together, in a Civil War year. Her husband has run off with the midwife, her two older sons are dead in the war, and now her youngest son, Perce, has just run off to join the Union army, much against her wishes. She has entertained him since he was a baby by telling him strange folktales and twisted old stories. Now she is alone.

MRS. WELSH: Once upon a time in the old, old time there was a woman lived alone in the middle of the dark woods. She had a husband, who run off, and three sons who went to be soldiers, and the first boy died, and the second boy died, and when the third boy went off, and she was alone, this woman stayed in the deep, dark woods and told herself stories, and one night she dreamed herself a dream about a big white house in the woods, like Mr. Lincoln's house in Washington, only bigger, and it was drafty, and eerie, with stairways and passages, and God lived in the big old house, and he looked out the windows, and saw the wilderness around him, all twisted and brown, and there was crows in the dead pumpkin fields, and it was cold, and everything was dying, and there was nothing to be done about it, so God closed up his windows and went fishing, and waited for somebody to come and ask him a question, and when she woke up from her dream she knew that her last son was a dead man, too, and she wandered out into the woods and sat under a walnut tree like an old goblin egg, and she never did move again, and she was ate up by the loneliness, and the wind came and blew all the leaves away, and there was nothing. *(The light fades on her.)*

GOING TO ST. IVES
Lee Blessing

Dramatic
Cora Gage, forties to fifties

> *Cora is a British doctor, here talking to the mother of a nefarious*
> *African dictator who has come to her for treatment of her failing*
> *eyesight. The woman has asked Cora to tell her why she became a*
> *doctor.*

CORA: I loved life. . . .

No. I loved life. That which animates. That first wriggle, that shiver.
The instant something turns into a living being. Indefinable. I get
the sheerest pleasure simply from its presence. . . .

There's nothing without life. They sent a mission to Mars —
utterly extraordinary, a different *world* — yet only one question interested us: Is there life? As though it couldn't be a world otherwise.
That fantastically pitiful picture of a tiny shovel sifting through a bit of
sterile dirt. *Please*, we thought, let there be mold, virus, something . . .
that on some level goes through what we do — lives, experiences, dies.
I don't know what we were going to do: put a leash 'round its neck,
give it a name? Still, it meant everything. When we found nothing,
centuries of fascination with the "Red Planet" simply vanished. Who
cares? No life. But then the meteorites in the polar ice cap were found,
and instantly the passion resumed — *ancient* life, microscopic, eons
ago. And we're spending trillions, just to know that once there had
been an organism there — the tiniest packet of matter — that was
alive. I for one understand that. That's how it is with me: personal,
visceral, irrational. I love life, I love to discover life, to save it. I love
to see it stay.

HER FIRST SCREEN TEST

Dan O'Brien

Seriocomic
Girl, twenties

> *In this monologue, originally produced at Actors Theatre of Louisville's Humana Festival (here printed in its entirety) an actress is apparently being taped by an (unseen) cameraman for some sort of screen test. She is in her dressing room at a theater.*

> *Dressing room, the Depression. A Girl enters, begins taking off her clothes.*

GIRL: We don't have much time. I'm the next act on stage. I was the vixen librarian, and now I'll be something new.

You'll see.

Just for you, first.

And then for them out there.

Are you shooting me already?

OK, here goes. *(She starts to undress.)*

Fuck!

— What?

Sorry, it's stuck!

I said, the Goddamned button —

— stuck on a Goddamned —

— See?

I've got this mouth on me. I'm sorry.

It's like a sewer, my father said. . . .

. . .

Hmm?

Of course it's a silent film.

What other kind of film is there? I can say whatever I Goddamn please!

(Her button comes undone.)

— Praise Jesus! *(Taking off her blouse.)*

I'm really a funny girl at heart.

A funny, religious girl.

A funny religious girl who happens to be burdened with a splendid body.

It's not easy being splendid: *(Taking off her skirt.)*

You've got more to lose that way.

And no one wants a funny girl to be pretty, anyway, it's an obstacle to ambition.

— Hmm?

. . .

Oh: My ambition is to be a star, of course.

To become a star of the vode-veal stage, and then:

Go legit.

Hit the silver screen.

Which is where you come in, my new friend . . .

My shy new man friend . . .

Tell me something: Do you really think I stand a chance?

. . .

Thanks.

. . .

Thank you.

. . .

Thanks so much for choosing me.

. . .

— More?

Can I turn around at least. *(She does.)*

. . . Don't the Injuns — ?

I said, the Indians have a theory that a person's picture steals her soul.

But I don't think that's true.

It's when I step out on stage that I feel that I'm dead . . .

It's crazy, I just know that I'm dead . . .

I mean, it doesn't mean anything if no one remembers you, after . . .

— Oh.

Sorry, yes, no I didn't mean —.

Of course not — !

You're an artist!
You're just doing your job!
— What do I look like to you?

. . .

. . .

. . .

. . .

. . .

. . .

Does it sound like I'm crying?
I'm changing, that's all.
— I've changed.
Let's see if you recognize me now. . . .

IS SHE IZZY OR IS HE AIN'TSY OR IS THEY BOTH

Lonnie Carter

Comic
Choo-Choo/Isabella, any age

> *This monologue is from a screwball murder mystery resolving the*
> *death of Isabella Borgward, at the hands, perhaps, of Justice "Choo-*
> *Choo" Justice. This play has been performed by high school and col-*
> *lege students and professionals. In other words, youngsters or*
> *anywhere up. This monologue follows shortly after the Courtroom*
> *Denouement in which it is revealed that Choo-Choo and Isabella*
> *are one and the same — sort of. Suzy Quzer, Isabella's Girl Thurs-*
> *day and Choo-Choo/Isabella have temporarily escaped the long arm*
> *of A. T. "Ernie" Law and are discovered by us. They are drinking.*

CHOO-CHOO/ISABELLA: It's no use, Suzy. They'll get me sooner or later. This is no life for a drunk like you, running away from the law, never knowing where the next shot's coming from. What you need is a dependable fellow to bring home the Cold Duck. Why don't you marry a bartender, settle down and raise stools. Get yourself a little blue heaven with mahogany pinball machines, a little sawdust to temper the vomit, that old Monroe calendar with James himself in the nude. There's a life for you, Suzy, a rail to hang on. With peanuts for lunch, Slim Jims for dinner — ah, Suzy, you'll be dead in a year. And all this time, Suzy, you thought I was Isabella. Well, so did I, Suzy, until one day I said, "Take off that wig, you dumb broad. You're not Izzy." And there I was. Ain'tzy. I mean Choo-Choo. A new me. But, it wasn't long I doubted the new me was me. Maybe the real me was she. Ah yes, she the she-me was the real me. But, I didn't like me being she. Me didn't either. So me and I talked of killing she. Me and I couldn't agree more on killing she, but how we could agree less on how I knew not. But I did know Kknot. Thoo' me knew Kknot not. I and me

25

would trick Kknot into thinking that she was dead. And you know the rest. But even if I had tricked Kknot into thinking she-I was dead, she-I wouldn't have been dead. It would have been a trick, which means that she-I does not not exist, does it not. Have I solved a knotty problem Suzy. But now what about the Kknotty problem. I don't know that, but I do know this. I'm either Izzy or I'm Ain'tzy, but what if I'm both.

(Singing.)

Iz I Izzy or iz I Ain'tzy or iz I both
Iz I Izzy or iz I Ain'tzy — I'll take an oath
I don't know
I'd like to have a baby
A lass or a little laddie
But when it saw its mommy, wouldn't it say "daddy"?

But don't you call me neuter
I may be one
I may be the other
But one thing's sure
If you call me "mister"
You're talking to a sister
Who's my brother

Which goes to show . . . I don't know . . . what I'd show . . . if I showed it . . .

JUMP/CUT
Neena Beber

Seriocomic
Karen, twenties

> *Karen has just been asked by her boyfriend, Paul, to move in with him. Here, she gives him her decision.*

KAREN: I'm sorry, but I don't think moving in together is a see-how-it-goes proposition. I think it's a turn my life upside-down, put my faith and my hope and my esteem in the hands of another human being, sacrifice my independence and my freedom and my self-sufficiency which I am willing to do on a leap, as an act of faith, an act of belief, but not as a dare or a gamble or a see-how-it-goes what-the-fuck. . . .

(A pop of light. Karen faces us. To audience.) I always wanted to be one of those what-the-hell girls . . . you know the ones I mean . . . they usually have a little tattoo of, say, a dolphin on their ankle that they got on the spur of the moment when it was trendy, what the hell. They smoke cigs and drink too much, what the hell. They've all been with other women, even the straight ones, what the hell. They're sexy, despite their usually stringy hair and unmade-up faces, because they think they are, and they're young as shit, and skinny, and they live with this guy and then that guy without losing faith, or innocence, or pride, what the hell great way to save on rent and hey, it's fun for a while, cool and carefree and shit I am just not, have never been, carefree.

(A pop of light as Karen returns to the scene with Paul. To Paul.) I will move in with you, Paul, what the hell. Until I can find my own place at least. But I want you to know that I didn't ruin a romantic moment. It was more like a toaster-oven moment. A blender moment. A perfectly utilitarian non-moment. OK?

KID-SIMPLE
Jordan Harrison

Seriocomic
Moll, a teenager

> *Moll is a gifted scientist who has invented a bizarre listening de-*
> *vice she calls The Third Ear. She is telling off Garth, a scruffily at-*
> *tractive boy who she thought was interested in her romantically, but*
> *who is in fact some sort of secret agent in the employ of Mysterious*
> *Parties who want her machine for their own nefarious ends. Garth*
> *has stolen the machine.*

MOLL: *(Barely scrutable.)* Goooaway. You're the ENEMY. . . .

Used to be I was your sun and moon and stars. What happened
to that? . . .
(Pause.)

I will get you for this, Garth. The world will have to go without new inventions for some time, because all my ingenuity will be
directed toward your undoing. I will GET you for messing with my
machine and my sanity. . . .

All of CREATION will get you. You will be FOOD. A plane
will drop you over the unforgiving Serengeti with a faulty parachute
an empty canteen no sunblock, and when one of these circumstances
fells you, you will finally do some good on this planet as recycled
material. Your meat will invigorate the ecosystem, your stumpy remains will feed the beasties of the earth. . . .

Lions, tigers, big sharks.

Crocs and bears and mean mean dogs —

What does it matter, don't interrupt! . . .

Unprotected from the African sun, your eyes will shrivel into
tiny raisins, the albino kind no one favors. And you will be alone,
totally alone, for so long that proximity to another body is *novel.* And

when you think you'll never see a human face again, I'll swoop in, *deus ex machina,* to say simply: 'Sup.

Your stumpy remains are so glad to see me, looking up to me like a God. But instead of kisses or cool clear water I serve you up a subpoena, bringing to the fore your crimes against United States patent law.

MAY ALL THIS COME TO PASS. The loneliness most of all.

KID-SIMPLE
Jordan Harrison

Comic
Moll, a teenager

> *Moll is a gifted scientist who has invented a bizarre listening device she calls The Third Ear. She is something of a geek in the romance department. Here, she is talking to a rather scruffily attractive boy named Garth, who has clearly come on to her.*

> *(In the following, Moll's interior thoughts are indicated by italics. Different and reverberant, these might be prerecorded, or spoken into a microphone. Still, the overall effect should be a seamless current of speech.)*

MOLL: *Back in my room I was safe I was safe and now here I am in his clutches but this is what you wanted didn't you want to know what it feels* like your place a lot, Garth. The Screeching Weasel poster really cozies it up, even if the feng shui could be *better be gentle, he'd better. I'm not one of those smitten by the brute, by the boot, thanks Sylvia Plath, but no thanks* for dinner! I've never had buffalo wings with ranch dressing before, is that a regional delicacy or *what is that rather unpleasant boy-musk is* that cologne you're wearing or what *IS that? probably he slaps a pint of horse piss under his pits every morning before heading out to tear the wings off ladybugs that's what boys do* you think it's hot in here? it seems hot but maybe I just have bad circulation in my extremities it isn't good for the blood to *Stop talking stop talking this instant stop. . . .*

> *Better take care, you better be delicate. Ms. Hanrahan in Sex Ed said it's like a beautiful flower opening inside you but she was probably ordered to say that or else the species would cease to put babies on this* earth feels like it's spinning faster than normal or is it just me *thinks the curious contortions of the human body are not for me, I fear I live in fear last chance to run to get me to a nunnery go! . . .*

But he's certainly All right *in the hospitality department maybe you haven't been fair probably he had a maladjusted childhood not everyone has fireside radio family time probably he had a stutter and that's why he doesn't venture words containing more than one syll—*

KIMBERLY AKIMBO
David Lindsay-Abaire

Comic
Pattie, midthirties

> *Pattie is the mother of a teenaged girl who has a disease that causes*
> *her to prematurely age. Pattie is pregnant again, and she is talking*
> *to her unborn child in her womb here.*
>
> *(Lights up on a tape recorder on a kitchen table. Pattie, in her mid-*
> *thirties, sits at the table. She wears a housecoat, slippers and she is*
> *very pregnant. Her hands are wrapped in bandages. Except for the*
> *light over the table, the kitchen is dark. It's late. Pattie looks at the*
> *tape recorder.)*

PATTIE: OK, here we go. Let's see. Record. *(She tries to press record, but her bandages are too big. She tries again.)* Jesus. How am I supposed to —? *(She tries with her elbow, her knee, her head, her nose, etc. Trying with her chin:)* Ow — I can't — stupid piece of crap — *(Click. Pattie sits up in disbelief. It's recording. She's winded but pleasantly surprised. She leans over and speaks into the recorder sweetly.)* Hello, darling. This is your mother speaking. You're in my belly right now. And sometimes you kick me. Isn't that precious? Now listen to me, sweetheart, because people are going to tell you awful things about me. You mustn't believe them. People lie. They are hateful cocksuckers. All of them. People spread vicious lies when victims aren't around to defend themselves. Remember that when I'm dead and someone tells you I was a demonic bitch. You stand up and tell them that I was sweet and funny and you have the tapes to prove it. It's always good to have evidence, sweetheart. That's why I'm making you this tape. I wanna make sure you get your info from the horse's mouth, because I'm gonna drop dead any second. *(Beat.)* On the bright side, I just got my carpal tunnel operation, so I may be able to use my hands before I die. We'll see. All those years in Secaucus took their toll. Sixteen years I worked in the Sunshine Cupcake Factory, pumping cream into those Ding-Dong knockoffs. Sixteen years of squeezing that Goddamn cream gun. That's one of the reasons we moved away from Secaucus. Not the *main* reason, but one of them. *(Beat.)* I hope I get to breast-feed. That's my one wish. If I give birth to you and they let me breastfeed, then I can die happily. I didn't get to do that with your sister. She was so bad off when she came out that they took her straight to I.C.U. They say that mother-child bond is so important, and it starts that very first moment. But she was never placed on my chest, and I never cooed over her, and she was never breast-fed, so I think we never had that. The bond thing.

KIMBERLY AKIMBO
David Lindsay-Abaire

Seriocomic
Pattie, midthirties

> *Pattie is convinced she's going to die soon, and is here breaking the news to her sister, Debra, and her teenaged daughter, Kimberly, who has a disease that causes premature aging.*

PATTIE: . . . I'm sorry I forgot, honey. I think the cancer's spread to my memory cells. . . . I'm gonna die, Kim. It's sad, but you need to be prepared. People pass away, you know. Suddenly they're gone forever. Look at Mr. Hicks. One day he's bringing me cabbages from his garden, the next day he drops dead. *(To Debra who passes from basement to exit house.)* Remember when Mr. Hicks dropped dead, Debra? . . . *(To Kimberly.)* You'll miss me, too. Because I'm a fixture in your life. You'll have to actually remind yourself I'm gone. That's how it was when your Nana died. I kept forgetting she was dead. I'd see a sale at the supermarket and think, "Oh Ma should get down there for those pork chops." And then I'd remember, "Oh yeah, she's dead." You get so used to someone being there, it takes your body a long time to adjust. *(Kimberly continues to clear the table.)* Like when you move a lamp, and you keep going to the same place to turn it on in the dark, even though you moved it across the room weeks ago. Or do you remember when Cinnamon died, and we still kept going to put the table scraps into his dog bowl? We were just so used to it? That's how it's gonna be when I'm gone. You'll have to keep reminding yourself that I'm not here anymore.

LIVING OUT
Lisa Loomer

Dramatic
Sandra, twenties/forties

> *Sandra is a Hispanic woman who works as a nanny. Here, she is sitting in a park talking to other Hispanic nannies as they watch their charges, about a confrontation she recently had with the father of her own child.*

SANDRA: Ay, mija, I never love nobody like I love this man! *(Makes the sign of the cross.)* God forgive me, not even the husband I got now. *(To baby.)* I love you, Jackson, but not like this! . . .

We was going to get married! En Oaxaca. Then, when I was three months pregnant, he say his mother don't want him to marry me 'cause he's Christian and I'm Catholic, and he give me money for the abortion, fijate! And when my son was born, my father give me money to leave Mexico — rapido! — and I had to leave my son and come here. Hijole, I cried for months, for years! . . .

Then last week, I talked to my cousin in Oaxaca, and she say he moved to Texas. So I called his house, his girlfriend answered the phone — *(Laughs.)* she called me a puta, la, la, la . . . But I I got dressed real nice and I took a picture of my son in his uniform — from the Catholic School — And I went to Texas . . .

(Seventeen years of emotions begin to well up and pour out of her. With laughter, pain, triumph.) And I tell him, "You know what? I have your son!" He thought I come for the child support, but I say — "I'm not after you! I have a happy life and I feel so proud of myself 'cause I got my citizenship now and I sent for our son!" And I showed him his picture! *(With sudden fierceness.)* I say, "I didn't ask for welfare and I didn't be a prostitute, and I didn't ask you for nothing! I didn't ask you — or my father — nobody! I just work every day and I feel so . . . with my face up." And then I left. He want to take me out to eat, but I say, "No, I'm really happy to see you and I just come to say hi."

LIVING OUT
Lisa Loomer

Dramatic
Ana, probably early to midthirties

> *Ana is a Hispanic woman who's living in California, where she
> works as a nanny. She is talking on the phone to her young son,
> Tomas, who lives back home with his grandmother while Ana and
> her husband try to get established in America.*

ANA: Tomas? Soy mami! . . . Me puedes oir, mijo? . . . Como estas? . . .
Si? Recibiste el paquete? And the shirt? Does it fit? *(Pronouncing it
for him.)* "Hill-finger." *(Laughs.)* I don't know, mijo, they like to put
their name on everything, quien sabe . . . How is school? . . . Then
you got to study a little harder, Tomas, so when you come here you
know your math . . . OK, just spend a little more time . . . What
are you eating? . . . Bueno, Tomas, pero don't eat too much sugar . . .
Pues, tell me something else — *(He's running out of conversation.)* Do
you miss me? . . . I miss you up to the sky! . . . You're going to come
real soon, mijo. *(Surprised.)* No, no, not for vacation — you're going
to come here to live! . . . No, not with abuela. Your great grandmother
don't want to come, mijo, she says she's too old. *(Pained.)* I know
it's hard to leave her. But don't you want to be with mami? . . . Oye,
did you get the pictures I sent you from the beach? With the rides?
(Laughs.) Te gustan? That's me and my sister-in-law and her friend.
(Pause; fighting tears.) No, mijo . . . I'm the one in the middle. *(She
hangs up.)*

THE LOVE SONG OF J. ROBERT OPPENHEIMER

Carson Kreitzer

Dramatic
Lilith, any age

> *This fascinating, surreal play is about the father of the atomic bomb. Lilith is a primeval goddess figure who flits in and out of, and comments on, the action. Here, she is responding to Oppenheimer's torment about the destructive force he is working to unleash.*

LILITH: I've heard all this sssssomewhere before.
    God says
    I've got this great idea
    I'm going to make a woman
    out of dirt
    and breathe into her nostrils and look how beautiful
    SHE LIVES.
    Adam and Lilith, my playthings. I breathed my wet god-breath into
    their little dirt mouths and look at the mud things walking around
    naming the beasts, eating the plants.

    then Adam says to me LIE DOWN
    as if we were not both the same
    he says LIE DOWN I WANT TO
    and I say, hey, wait a minute here, I'm not saying let's not have fun,
    but what makes you the one to climb up on top of me? I don't think
    this is really about sex here I don't think this is about exploring these
    new bodies with the new wet life breathed in I think this is about
    you trying to get on top of me
    LIE DOWN
    I think you want to hold me there
    LIE DOWN

He would not stop saying it and his face all red
LIE DOWN
Grabbed both my arms and tried to knock me down in the dirt we'd
both come from.

I spoke the sacred name of God and flew up into the sky.

Went off on my own, to the shores of the red sea. Till he thought
better of his behavior.
We're all learning here, after all.

But Adam
Adam goes to God and he complains
that I will not lie down and God says

What?

Don't worry, little man
I will make you a new one.

I will rip open your side.

and take from you

since you would not take what I made you the first time

(and I thought, made You?)

let me rip a piece from you
close to the heart

now I take this dripping bloody piece of you and I make you a woman
who will lie down. She will do nothing but lie down.
she will lie down for you.

and to me he says

eat their babies.
They are delicious.

Especially the red-brown marrow in the troughs of their white bones.

THE LOVE SONG OF J. ROBERT OPPENHEIMER

Carson Kreitzer

Dramatic
Kitty, thirties to forties

> *Kitty is the wife of J. Robert Oppenheimer, the father of the atomic*
> *bomb, who is in a congressional committee room, where he is being*
> *grilled by congressman intent on finding communist infiltration in*
> *the government.*

KITTY: Bastards.
Bastards.
Bastards.

D'you hear that, Joe Dallet? You and your Goddamned Party. Your
sleek, incomparable ideals. And I fell for you. In my bright party dress.
And then there were no more party dresses, just the Party. Hardly
any dresses at all. Left behind comfort and ease, and that vague sense
of unease that comes with. Left behind my family's money, as you
had. Fighting for the Worker. Fighting against your Father and his
fat money, money made striding over the backs of the poor. I fell
for you and your sweet rightness, and love was enough for anything.
Married in a plain blue dress at City Hall, and love was enough for
anything. Living in a one-room flat with tenement heat and five cent
meals in the greasy restaurant downstairs, because the stove leaked
and might blow us all up. And love was not enough, Joe. I went back
to my family. I missed hot water, and pretty clothes, and steak. And
college. So I went back. Sat in that big living room in my pretty dress
and the unease settling like an angry saint on my shoulders. Didn't
know Mother was intercepting your letters. I thought you were dis-
gusted with my weakness. Finally I broke, wrote begging you to take
me back. By then you were fighting fascists in Spain. Said you'd never

stopped loving me a day. We were to meet in Paris but instead I got the telegram. And the official condolences of the Goddamned Party. *(Smokes.)*

A dead man is no good to me, Joe.

Pretty speeches and pretty ideals. You bled to death on a field in Spain. Stalin did not feed his people. There is no free state for the worker.

A dead man is no good to me, Joe. I'll take a gin martini any day. And the love of a man who is here. With his arms around me. At the head of our table, with our children. Leaning down to kiss the top of my hair. You'd like him, Joe. I know you would. You would say he's good for me.

Do you hear that? In there?
They're killing him.
This will kill him.

Right now they're asking him about me. His wife and her Party Membership. If he muttered Atomic Secrets in his sleep, would I pass them along to Mother Russia.

(Smokes.)

Mother Russia. If I ever see the old bitch I'll scratch her eyes out. Tell her to stop killing
my men.

MY SWEETHEART'S THE MAN IN THE MOON

Don Nigro

Seriocomic
Evelyn, twenty-eight

> *Evelyn Nesbit, a celebrated American beauty, around 1906, seated on a bench at the center of the stage, in a circle of light, surrounded by darkness. First the mistress of the celebrated architect Stanford White, then the wife of mentally disturbed millionaire Harry Thaw, her life will be ruined when Thaw shoots White in the head one night at the theater. The light flickers on her, as if she were an image in an old movie. She is very young, fragile looking, and quite exquisitely beautiful.*

EVELYN: There's a movie about me at the Nickelodeon,
and one at the vaudeville house.
I am the youngest and most beautiful
of the world famous Floradora Sextette.
I am the girl on the polar bear rug.
I am the Gibson Girl, and the Eternal Question.
I should be on the stage, they said.
Men said this. Men say these things.
It means they want to see you naked.
Are there any more at home like you, my dear?
they said. No. I'm the only one.
At the top of Madison Square Garden
we'd hang on the naked moon goddess,
and look down at New York in the night.
When I woke up, I was naked.
He pushed me naked on a red velvet swing
and the painted toenails of my little bare feet
pierced the flowered Japanese parasol

on the ceiling. I felt weightless at the top.
His apartment was full of mirrors.
He wanted me so naked.
I wasn't even wearing hairpins.
Now you belong to me, he said.
I have fallen into an abyss of moral turpitude.
My God, Harry, I said. What have you done?
I kissed him on the elevator after.
His mouth smelled like peppermints.
My sweetheart's the man in the moon.

MY SWEETHEART'S THE MAN IN THE MOON

Don Nigro

Dramatic
Evelyn, late teens/early twenties

> *Evelyn Nesbit, the most celebrated beauty of her time, has had her*
> *life turned hopelessly upside down when her insane husband, the*
> *millionaire Harry Thaw, murders her ex-lover, the famous archi-*
> *tect Stanford White, in front of several hundred people at the the-*
> *ater and then, after his incarceration in an asylum, escapes and shows*
> *up one night in Evelyn's bed. The year is 1913. Evelyn is twenty-*
> *eight. Here, in her bedroom, Evelyn, nearly at the end of her rope,*
> *finally gives vent to her pent up feelings of anger and frustration as*
> *she tries to convince Harry, his horrible and manipulative wealthy*
> *mother, and her crooked lawyers to leave her alone.*

EVELYN: Harry, what are you doing here?
You're supposed to be in the madhouse.
Are you crazy? You can't be here.
Harry, you've got to get out of here. I can't have
an escaped lunatic in my bedroom.
What are you people trying to do to me?
Your mother gives me just enough to live on
so I'll keep coming to your sanity hearings
and saying you're all better, and meanwhile
you escape and crawl in my bedroom window.
What the hell is the matter with you people?
Just who the hell do you people think you are?
You think you own everything and everybody.
You own newspapers and history books and laws
and crooked sticky-fingered governors
and crooked sticky-fingered presidents

and crooked sticky-fingered lawyers
who threaten and humiliate and bully
and buy the truth, buy everybody's souls.
You've taken everything I've got, but you
can't have my soul. It's mine. My soul is mine.

NECESSARY TARGETS
Eve Ensler

Dramatic
Jelena, twenties to thirties

> Necessary Targets *is about an encounter group organized by two American volunteers to help Bosnian women who are victims of the terrible conflict there. Jelena, one of the refugees, is here talking to other members of the group.*

JELENA: I was so happy last night, alive like I used to be before. I woke Dado to dance, to dance with me. He had been drinking and he'd passed out. But this did not stop me. I felt light-headed and full of a kind of perfect faith, full of God. "Dado," I said last night, "Dado, you must get up and dance with me under the stars, rise up, re-member." And I must have pulled at him roughly, and I frightened him and he just went mad, screaming about not taking him outside, the knives, how he'd do anything, not to hurt him, not to hurt the others — his father, that was his father, to stop with the knives, stop carving his father, his fingers, his chest, his father. To stop. And he started begging, crying like a little boy, and when he found himself all little on the ground, broken, hating that I loved him, he beat me. But I felt nothing. Nothing. Dado's fists, they could not touch me. I was with the old Dado. This new one, this new mutation of war, could not invade my happiness, could not invade my great dance under the stars.

NECESSARY TARGETS
Eve Ensler

Dramatic
Zlata, twenties to thirties

> Necessary Targets *is about an encounter group organized by two*
> *American volunteers to help Bosnian women who are victims of the*
> *terrible conflict there. Zlata is a member of that group, here talk-*
> *ing to one of the American volunteers about what happened in her*
> *country.*

ZLATA: It's Bosnia. The song of Bosnia, the world of Bosnia that flows cold
clean in the stream and tastes like a full meal. Bosnia, the kindness
we shared, how we lived in each others' warm kitchens, in sunny cafes,
in the room of Bosnia. My room. Gone. Blown to bits and pieces. It
isn't the cruelty that broke my heart. Cruelty is easy. Cruelty like stu-
pidity is quick, immediate. They break in, they wear masks, they smell
bad, they have machetes, they chop off the heads of my old parents
sitting on their couch. There is blood, lots of it. There is screaming.
There are dead headless bodies. Cruelty is generic. Cruelty is boring,
boring into the center of the part of you that goes away — we are
dead, all of us, to the suffering. There is too much of it. But remind
us of the beauty, the beet fields in full bloom, the redness of the fields.
Remind us how we once sang, how the voices echoed as one through
the landscape of night and stars. Remind us how often we laughed,
how safe we felt, how easy it was to be friends. All of us. I miss everything — Bosnia was paradise.

NO SOLICITING
Shel Silverstein

Comic
Nellie, twenties to forties

> *Nellie's rant is about a disappointing relationship she had with a*
> *man in the past. She's talking to Ed, a potential prospect.*

NELLIE: I could have used a sign . . . that said . . . "Talk to me, Jim" —
and he could have used a sign that said "What's there to say, Nellie?"
And I could have used a sign that said "There must be something to
say." I'm — we're living . . . we're doing *something* . . . let's talk about
what we're doing . . . We're not doing anything. Well, Jim, let's talk
about what we're not doing — let's talk about what we . . . might have
done — Turn on the TV, Nellie. I don't want to watch TV, Jim — Turn
on the TV, Nellie . . . I want to talk, Jim. . . .

Son-of-a-bitchin' bastard . . . *(Pause.)* Son of a bitchin' bastard . . .
Keep off . . . Keep out . . . Beware . . .

Bastard beware . . . explosives . . . ha . . . you don't have that one
— You don't have any of those — what good are you? You're not current — you're not up-to-date . . . up-to-the-minute . . . you've got
to be . . . current . . . that's what he told me — well, he won't have
to worry. About that — stop . . . I could have used a stop sign. But
it wouldn't have helped. You can't teach another old dog — "Beware
of the Dog." Too late — too late — *(She sings.)* "Yes my heart belongs to . . ." did you hear something? . . . I thought I . . . "Yes my
heart belongs to Daddy — Da-da-da-da-da-da-dad. So I want to warn
you laddie" — Not you — it's part of the song. *(Talks.)* "So I want
to warn you laddie, though I know you're perfectly swell, my heart
belongs to Daddy, cause my Daddy he treats it so well." They don't
write songs like that . . . now . . . Now you hear garbage and obscenity.
Loud . . . Loud garbage. Loud obscenity. *(Quiet sigh.)* Too late, all
too late — Do you have one that says *"Too Late"* or . . . *"I'm Sorry."*

I'll buy that one. "I'm *Sorry*," I am you know *(She peeks at sign.)* "Help"? That's one I could have used — "Help." . . .

"Help Wanted." Yes — but *wanted* — past tense. No it's just . . . what? . . . what's wanted now? . . . Peace? I don't know. . . .

You know what else was wanted? Past tense — wanted — an entire lifetime . . . conversation. Signs. What kind of a day did you have? I had a lovely day, Jim. I tied the tomatoes and I put up some green beans and I took a nice long walk to the bridge and back. The leaves were turning, Jim. What did they look like, Nellie? *Flaming* — orange and red and yellow — on fire — let's talk about it. Jim . . . Come on, Jim. We can talk about it no. We have signs — I love you, Nellie — I love you, Jim . . . What? . . . Did you say something? . . .

Too late — another time will be . . . there'll be a "Too Late" sign on the door . . . somebody else's. Will have sold it to me . . . too late . . . "Closed" . . . "No Trespassing" . . . "House for Sale . . ." . . .

You'll come back to shuttered windows . . . Dusty doors and shuttered windows — Do doors get dusty? *Rusty* rusty hinges . . . *Rooms* get dusty . . . Rooms with furniture covered with sheets — to keep the dust off — what's under the sheets? Is it . . . it . . . or is it a who? You can't tell . . . people can look a lot like furniture . . . I did — I became furniture — Don't ever turn your — Are you married? . . .

Don't ever turn your wife into furniture. Promise me you never will.

PALESTRINA
Don Nigro

Comic
Becky Reedy, nineteen

> *Becky Reedy, age nineteen, a thin, pretty girl, sits on a porch step of the Palestrina house in Armitage, a small town in the hilly section of east Ohio in the year 1946, not feeling well at all. Her new boyfriend, Johnny Palestrina, a young veteran of World War II, has just brought her home to meet his large family of Italian Catholics, immigrants from southern Italy. Becky is a Protestant girl, a descendant of east Ohio pioneers, and is very much out of her element with these people. She is also by nature nervous and troubled, already has two illegitimate children by a carnival man, and is desperate to make a good impression. But she's not used to drinking Mr. Palestrina's homemade wine, and she has just been violently throwing up her lasagna in the bushes. She is speaking to Johnny's tough Italian mother, Anna Palestrina, who has taken her outside to care for her while she's being sick. Becky knows Anna doesn't approve of her.*

BECKY: Oh, God. I want to die. I just want to die. . . . Yes I do. I really do. I've never thrown up so much in my life. I thought I was never going to stop. I think I puked up some stuff I ate when I was twelve. . . .

    Oh, no, no, the lasagna was wonderful. That's why I ate so much. It wasn't the lasagna, it was the wine. Not that the wine wasn't great. The wine was super. That's why I drank so much. . . .

    I just didn't realize it was such strong stuff. Your husband tried to warn me, but it was so good, it tasted like really incredibly good grape juice, like at Communion at the Christian Church. . . .

    It's a Protestant thing, I guess. And I was so nervous when I got here, I mean. I stepped on the cat and knocked over the hat rack and everything, and the wine made me feel so relaxed and happy, and the lasagna was so good, I ate way too much, way too fast, and then your kitchen started spinning around like carousel horses and the next thing I knew, I was sitting on your sister Lucrezia's lap. God. Poor Johnny. You must think he brought home the dumbest girl in the state of Ohio. . . .

I'm really sorry. I mean, I'm so sorry. You must really hate me.

PALESTRINA

Don Nigro

Comic
Becky Reedy, nineteen

> *Becky Reedy, age nineteen, a thin, pretty girl, sits on a porch step of the Palestrina house in Armitage, a small town in the hilly section of east Ohio in the year 1946, not feeling well at all. Her new boyfriend, Johnny Palestrina, a young veteran of World War II, has just brought her home to meet his large family of Italian Catholics, immigrants from southern Italy. Becky is a Protestant girl, a descendant of east Ohio pioneers, and is very much out of her element with these people. She is also by nature nervous and troubled, already has two illegitimate children by a carnival man, and is desperate to make a good impression. But she's not used to drinking Mr. Palestrina's homemade wine, and she has just been violently throwing up her lasagna in the bushes. She is speaking to Johnny's tough Italian mother, Anna Palestrina, who has taken her outside to care for her while she's being sick. Becky knows Anna doesn't approve of her.*

BECKY: Really, you don't have to be so nice to me. I know you don't want me seeing your son. I know you think I'm just some stupid farm girl with two children and a dead husband. . . .

June is three and Lorry is two. . . .

My aunt Liz has them today. She raised me. I'm an orphan, sort of. Sometimes my aunt Moll takes them. . . .

And they like him. God, they love him. They like him better than they like me. . . .

It's true. Well, he likes them better than I do. What I mean is, he's not stuck with them all the time, so it's easier for him to like them. Not that I'm not a good mother. It's just that they drive me crazy. June is very serious, she just stares at me, you just want to throw the telephone at her or something, and Lorry is, God, Lorry is like a whole army of little girls, she's demented quadruplets on drugs, I can't shut her up. I can't keep track of her, she's into everything, it's horrible. The other day I found her in the bread box naked. She goes to the refrigerator and opens the door, takes out all the eggs and throws them against the wall. She gets up in the middle of the night and turns on the radio as loud as it will go. Last night I woke up and thought Bing Crosby was in bed with me. I don't know how you Italian people do it. I mean, you have such big families, but all your kids seem to have turned out great. Mine I think are going to grow up to be a store mannikin and a bank robber. What a nightmare. . . .

I'm a mess, aren't I? You really hate me a lot. . . .

You're not denying it. You talk about the guy blowing his nose on the bricks and you talk about the old guy burning his imaginary trash, but you don't deny it. Johnny told me how you want him to marry a nice Italian girl and all. Probably you're right. I mean, what does he want with somebody else's kids and a nineteen-year-old wife who throws up his mother's lasagna in the bushes for twenty minutes and steps on the cat?

PENDRAGON
Don Nigro

Dramatic
Isabel, late teens to early twenties

> *Isabel is a young Basque girl who has come to America from Gernika,*
> *Spain, in 1910 to marry her childhood sweetheart, Joe Navarro,*
> *whom she hasn't seen since they were children. But her boat sank in*
> *a storm on the way across the Atlantic, and Joe and his family in*
> *Boise, Idaho, believe she must have drowned. Now she's turned up*
> *in the train station in Boise, rather lost, a stranger in her new coun-*
> *try, and changed a bit by the trauma of the shipwreck. John Rhys*
> *Pendragon, a journalist in Boise to cover a prize fight, and an ac-*
> *quaintance of Joe's, has just helped rescue her from a religious lu-*
> *natic who has been making advances to her, and she's trying to explain*
> *to him how she got there.*

ISABEL: I took the boat. I rode on a cart from Gernika with my friend
Teresa's brother Felix, whose horse smelled terrible, but he was kind
to me and gave me a flower. Then I took the boat from Donostia and
we sailed on the ocean for a long time and white birds followed the
ship, and a family named Ascuenaga from Zarauz was nice to me,
and their little boy who had one eye was in love with me and would
go to sleep in my lap when I sang to him the song about the famous
country of France where the pig-doctors and scissors-grinders come
from, and one night when the captain was drinking and singing a
shameful song about someone named Barnacle Bill there was a terrible storm and the captain fell off the upper deck onto his head and
the ship turned sideways and broke apart and everybody drowned. . . .

No, I remember drowning. But then I woke up someplace else
where the beach was very shiny and there was a fort on a hill, and
some people took care of me and put me on another boat to a place
called New Orleans, and then I was on a train, and then another train,

and then I was misplaced for a while in Utah, and then they put me on another train and when I woke up the conductor said I was here, only now my husband doesn't want to marry me any more. . . .

Time doesn't matter. You learn this when you drown. There was a crazy Englishman who came to live in our town to write a book, and he played checkers with the priest and helped me learn English. He was trying to prove to us we were the lost people of Atlantis. He thought Basque was the language of the mermaids. . . .

This man had things missing in his brain and we all felt sorry for him, but he was a good teacher and gave me peppermints for my little sister, although he did swear at the priest when he lost at checkers, but when I was drowning there was a noise in my ears like somebody singing a song of ours about the Tree of Gernika, which is a very ancient tree in the town of Gernika where I live, and is very important to us, to my people, and I thought about the crazy Englishman with the peppermints and what he said about the mermaids, but if I told Joe he'd think I was insane because Basques don't talk like that, so maybe there are things missing from my brain, too, now, and I should have stayed in the ocean and drowned.

PRIVATE JOKES, PUBLIC PLACES
Oren Safdie

Dramatic
Margaret, twenties

> *Margaret is a gifted architectural student presenting her thesis project before a panel of faculty members who are to varying degrees skeptical and hostile, more interested in arguing about their own theories of architecture than in seriously evaluating Margaret's design, or listening to her own beliefs about architecture. After much kowtowing to them, Margaret finally speaks up about her design and about what architecture means to her.*

MARGARET: When I was two years old my family came to this country. We lived in a small apartment in a large building. You'd never see the same person twice. One summer my grandfather came to visit us from Korea. He was a famous Modern architect back home, and brought us lots of presents. I got a Lego set so I could learn to make buildings just like him. Immediately, I took the pieces out of the box and starting making all sorts of shapes. But my grandfather stopped me, and proceeded to show me how to make my building, stacking one piece on top of the other, much in the way the building I lived in was put together. That night, after he went to sleep, I switched on the night lamp and quietly started making a building the way I wanted to. I rotated one piece at 90 degrees and snapped it on to another so that one person's roof became another person's terrace. I made sure that every apartment had lots of light and that everyone had a garden. The next morning I was awakened by the sound of my grandfather taking my building apart. He then put all the pieces back in the box and I never saw them again. . . . On my first day in architecture school, my professor gave us an assignment: We had twenty-four hours to come up with a design for a poet's retreat. The site was on a hill, and we were given a whole list of requirements, including square footages and an approximate budget. As if I was a real architect, I sat down at my table and carefully measured out each room, calculating material costs, and trying to see how I could best utilize the site to maximize the views towards the valley. Later that night, deep into the project, I lifted my head for the first time and saw that nobody was obeying the rules. It was a spectacle, every project trying to outdo the other. One student had made a mobile that hung down from a man-made cliff, another had dug down two hundred feet, carving out a small island in the middle of a water well. When I asked whether they were worried about being penalized for not following the rules, they laughed at me. "Everyone knows rules are made to be broken," they said. And so, I started from scratch. I put trapdoors where there were supposed to be floors. I made a beautiful courtyard that could only be seen but never occupied, and finally I constructed a long plank that extended a hundred feet out, just in case the poet grew frustrated with life and wanted to kill himself . . . I got an A.

(Margaret starts to remove her rings, bracelets, sweater, and lets down her hair.)

Later that night, as I was getting ready for bed in my tiny dormitory room, I began to get an uneasy feeling in my stomach. It was as if I knew that someone, somewhere, had been cheated . . . You see, people don't care what philosophers we've studied or which computer graphics program we use. They don't care about Nietzche, Freud or for that matter Le Corbusier. What they do care about is what sort of environment they live in. They might not always be able to recognize what it is about a space that makes them feel comfortable or irritated . . . But I do know that the people who will come to use my swimming pool will come back to use it again. And I do know that it will make them feel a little better about life . . .

QUICK AND DIRTY
David Riedy

Seriocomic
Woman, any age

> *A guy meets this attractive woman on a subway platform, but she has quite a chip on her shoulder about men.*

WOMAN: Want to know what I was thinking, while we were exchanging looks? . . . *(Beat.)* I came down the stairs from the street, and nearly fell. I slipped on the front of a step, in a hurry because I didn't want to miss the train. I wanted to be home in my bathrobe, on the couch, drinking CranApple juice and doing the crossword. That's all I've thought about all day at work: "CranApple and crossword." There's no train. Instead, there's an announcement, a delay. I drop my briefcase and fall against the wall, worn out. More and more people arrive, lean against the wall. I watch, eyes half-closed, unamused. But then, an interesting man. Somewhat attractive. Black jeans, heavy boots — to be stylish, he doesn't do construction, that's obvious — he's an intellectual, or thinks he is. But he is attractive. His face has large, inviting, sensual features. Big, soft lips, a substantial nose. And his eyebrows intrigue me. They're very dark and thick, and lifted to an almost unbelievably cocky height. I imagine those eyebrows, pushed down in concentration, his whole face intent, as this man lays underneath me and carefully inserts his large — generously large — erect penis inside of me. I'm sitting back on my feet, balancing on the couch, my bathrobe untied and wide-open. A glass of CranApple and a yellow No. 2 pencil in my left hand. I take a gulp while you carefully maneuver your pelvis to rub nice and slow, and I look at my other hand, with the crossword in it, and 18-across is a nine-letter word ending with *n*. The clue is "the king was one," and as I look down at your sexy, bush eyebrows to tell you in a voice made deep by your "attentions" that the answer is "swordsman" . . . you walk up and interrupt me.

THE REEVES TALE
Don Nigro

Seriocomic
Abby, thirty-two

> *Abby is married to a farmer named Sim Reeves. Here, she is talking to a good-looking farmhand named John, who has asked her why a good-looking woman like her would marry a brutal man like Sim. Molkin is Abby's teenaged daughter.*

ABBY: I was at the Christian Girls' Camp, Molkin's age. Boys used to get drunk and come down to gawk at the girls on Saturday night, look in the windows. Most of the girls had rich parents from Cleveland and Akron, but this girlfriend of mine and I were sent up to the camp by our church in West Virginia, as a kind of charity thing. Sim would drive by in this awful old Chevy pickup truck with some other boys. They were older than us, and one day when some of us girls were skinny-dipping in the strip mine in the afternoon, that was the beginning of it. . . .

   We got caught in the water with our clothes on the bank and the boys sat on the rocks and struck up a conversation with us. There wasn't much we could do but sass them back. I wasn't scared. I knew I could handle those boys. They didn't look too awfully bright, and I'd got into camp in the first place because I was the smartest girl in Bible school. . . .

   We talked back and forth a while until it got kind of cold in the water and time we were getting back to the camp, so I swam around behind some rocks and tried to sneak up onto the shore, but Sim caught me. . . .

   I was all wet and full of goose pimples from the wind and he caught me by a row of poplar trees, and he was kissing me and pressing me against him and touching me and I guess I just decided it was something I wasn't going to waste, so we wrestled down into the high grass and the wind blowing in the poplars and I let him, and then I let him again, and pretty soon I was sneaking out nights with him, and it was so secret and wicked and the trees smelled so good. It was the best time in my life. . . .

Molkin makes noises in her sleep. It's like going to bed with a howler monkey. . . .

Sim thought I had money because the other girls did. He didn't know I was a charity case. He kept calling me his rich girl, and I knew he was after more than just my body, but I didn't want it to stop, so I just let him think what he pleased. I'd tell him I wasn't rich, and he'd say, I bet your daddy is, though, and I'd tell him my daddy raised pigs in West Virginia, but he thought I was teasing him. Then I got pregnant, and we ran off and got married, and he found out my folks were even poorer than his folks, and things kind of went down hill from then on. Now she's the same age I was then, only not as smart. She's half Sim, and he's mostly subhuman. But then, I guess I'm not so smart after all, to end up like this, am I? Sim won't pay you right. He'll find a way to cheat you. That's one thing he is smart about. He'll cheat you and call it business. He always finds a way. I was a baby when I married him. Now I'm thirty-two. . . .

I'm trying to make it go away. Maybe I'm trying to make YOU go away. How old are you? . . .

I think of you as a boy. I think of myself as if I was my mother when she was fifty. I watch television, Sim sits there slobbering over girls with no bras. My daughter wants to be one of those girls.

THE REEVES TALE
Don Nigro

Comic
Molkin Reeves, sixteen

> *In the autumn of 1972, Molkin Reeves lives with her family in two
> rooms of the now horribly decrepit old Pendragon mansion they rent
> in rural east Ohio, where some very strange and disturbing things
> have been happening — the trees are glowing and moving at night,
> there is a strange buzzing sound everywhere, something seems to be
> living in the attic, and her abusive, uncouth father has just disap-
> peared, possibly dragged down the well by something. To try and take
> her mind off these terrible events, Molkin is attempting to describe
> to what's left of her family what she has been learning about life in
> her biology class.*

MOLKIN: Frogs is amphipians. Learned that in biology. Now turtles, on
the other hand, is reptiles. They come after the amphipians. See, first
there was like fish, or, actually, first there was slime, and then there
was like jellyfish kinda crap, and then there was fish and stuff, and
then some of the fish they got together and got flung up onto the
land, you see, and they kinda liked it there, so they decided to grow
legs, so they could crawl around better in the mud, and so they became amphipians, and they would sorta commute from the water to
the mud and back, and some of them got tired of goin' back and forth
all the time so they just camped out right there in the mud, and them
was the reptiles, like dinosaurs and stuff, like Rex the Tyrannosaur
with the little tiny hands, who used to eat everybody, and the Brochial
Sores like on the cartoons with the long tails, and snakes, which is
reptiles that throwed away their arms and legs, and the turtles, which
grew houses on their backs so they could have someplace to hide right
there with them all the time. Now, amphipians lay their eggs in the
water, whereas the reptiles, they lays their eggs on the land and then

when the baby turtles hatch they gotta run like hell for the water so the birds don't get 'em, which don't make a whole lot of sense to me, but then, what does? And you know, Mama, the more I study in my biology, the more it seems to me that God must be some sort of a homicidal maniac, you know what I mean? Maybe one of them buzzards from Hinkley mistaked Daddy for a giant turtle and swupped him up and took him off to his mountain crag to feed him to his children, what do you think? See, buzzards is birds, of course, and the birds, they happened when some of the reptiles woke up and had feathers and discovered that if they jumped up in the air they could kinda hang there if they flopped their arms back and forth. See, the fish was kinda like the Navy, and the reptiles was the Army, and the birds was the Air Force, and the amphipians, they was the Marines, like Johnny. I want to go to the circus. Can I have a dollar to go see the elephants? Now, elephants is mammals, although they don't have much hair and they talk through their nose like the French, but they're very intelligent although I think we killed most of them to make pianos or something. Mammals is warm-blooded. That means they carry the heat inside them and hatch their eggs right inside the mother, see, and then give birth to them alive, which is a real mess, and they got to take care of their offspring for a very long time, or they die, like from, you know, lack of warmth. Mammal babies, they need lots of warmth. They need to be touched and held, or they just shrink up and die, from the cold. I like the circus because of the animals. I like all kinds of animals, especially the mammals, because of the warm nature of their bodies. It's just people I don't like very much. Of course, the problem with animals is, you get kinda attached to them, and they tend to croak on you. I guess no circus, huh?

REFUGEES
Stephanie Satie

Dramatic
Farideh, any age

> Refugees *is a play about a disparate group of refugees from the world's
> incessant conflicts who have come to the United States. It takes place
> in an English-as-a-foreign-language course, whose teacher has asked
> Farideh, an Iranian woman, to practice her English skills by telling
> her story.*

FARIDEH: I am Farideh. I, like Jilla, am also from Iran. But I am not married. I came from my country one year ago. I came illegally in a truck
tru Pakistan, hiding with the boys who don't want to go into the army
in the war with Iraq. I was the only girl. I loved my country. I came
because of what happened to my family. I was twelve years old when
there was revolution in my country, and, after two years they kill my
mom? She was working, she had beauty salon, and witout any, any
reason — nothing, they just kill her. One day somebody come to my
house and say to my dad that they took my mom at four o'clock —
and they don't know what happened to her. We were crazy looking
all over for her. At that time, in the morning, five o'clock every morning — all the people listening to the radio, because that's when they
say the names of the people that they kill the night before. You know?
That night they killed twenty-four people. They just kill them. They
did the court in the night and they killed twenty-four persons. But
we didn't listen to dis because we knew it wasn't possible. My mom
was pregnant. After that I see all these people coming to our house.
I say to the people that are coming "Why are you here?" They say,
"You don't know anything?"

They scared to tell us because my mom, she was so nice to everybody, you don't know, and all the people that they knew her they were
coming to our house, and we didn't know anything. My aunt, she

63

pick up the phone and call to the radio station and say, "Repeat again please the names of the people that were killed from last night."

Suddenly she just hang up the phone, and screaming in the house. The only person that they kill that was pregnant was my mom. You know she said, "I'm pregnant," but they didn't believe it and they didn't do the test and they kill her. And in that religion — in Islam — they can't kill a person that she's pregnant, by law, by religion law they can't do that. And after that, they come to our house . . . someone from the government come to take our house; to tell us we must leave this place. Because they kill her they have the right to take any property that's in her name. After that we went to Teheran to apply for a passport to leave Iran. You know, I was going for my passport, for like three years. They said "You cannot go; if you want to go, somebody in your family must stay and sign that you're going and will come back." This is for all Jewish people. They said, "You are nice girl; why you don't marry with Muslim man?" Finally I said to them, "If you don't want to give me passport, I will go illegally." That was the last day that I was in my country.

REFUGEES
Stephanie Satie

Dramatic
Larissa, any age

> Refugees *is a play about a disparate group of refugees from the world's*
> *incessant conflicts who have come to the United States. It takes place*
> *in an English-as-a-foreign-language course, whose teacher has asked*
> *Larissa, a Russian woman, to practice her English skills by telling*
> *her story.*

LARISSA: Oh, my God, it's impossible to speak after Farideh. All right, all
right, I will try. I am from Moscow. I just had job interview, but not
in my real profession. I have my degree in Divining Rod. You know
you can say where to put a bed in or a door so you don't get cancer.
The divining rod only works for those people who believe they can
contact the divine spirit through the medium of the person using the
rod. Unfortunately, there is not such great demand for this skill.

Look, I am all alone here so I'm always looking for best opportunity. For me, America, it's great adventure. When I was in Moscow,
I put out, you know, personal advertisement, and yes, I received quite
a few responses. Many American men are looking to marry Russian
women who want to come here because they know we are intelligent
and can work hard, but it's very difficult to know if what they tell
about themselves it's true. So, I met this man, and he seemed very
nice. He tells me he has a house, owns his own business, so it is approved by my government and I marry with him in Moscow. Then,
he returns to Cleveland, and when my papers are in order I fly to
Cleveland, stopping over for two hours in New York. But, just to be
on safe side, I contact other candidate with whom I have been cor-
responding. He lives in Los Angeles. I tell him I will be in JFK for
two hours on such and such a day, and, if he likes, we can meet. *(Nods
yes.)* Yes, he knows I've chosen other candidate and that I'm already

married, but, you know, you never know. So he comes to JFK for two hours. He is very old, seventy-five, but very nice, and he tells me that if it doesn't work out in Cleveland, that I should come to Los Angeles.

So, I fly to Cleveland and, oh my God, my husband tells me he has no money. He only permits me to take shower every four days because water is expensive. And we have to walk to and from supermarket. My dear, we are living in suburbs. It's two, three miles, and yes, of course he has car, but he doesn't want to spend money on gas. So, there's nothing I can do. If I divorce him, they'll send me back like that (*Snaps fingers.*) because I'm not refugee. I'm just here to get away from KGB. But that's other story.

So, I call Los Angeles and he says, OK, come, we'll see. So, now he is my like my landlord. I have my own room in his house. He feeds me, buys me cigarettes, teaches me driving and computer, and for now, it's OK. But he knows I have to have other husband lined up, ready to go, you know to the altar, minute I get divorced from other husband in Cleveland. So, I am looking.

THE ROOM FULL OF ANNIE

Annika Rosenvinge

Seriocomic
Annie, twenties

Annie wears a thick jean jacket over a nightgown. She is standing facing the audience. She is young and weary looking. There is something tense in the way she holds her shoulders, in how her arms are held around herself.

ANNIE: Hello again, all you. Hello brown hair. Hello glasses. Hello. It's so strange that I don't know your names. You're like the best friends I never had, so faithfully coming . . . every day. I used to run every day. I don't know, as you all know. All this flesh to waste. I do my best running when I'm alone. If I'm alone, I can stop thinking about how I am smiling or not smiling or how my thighs look or if people are looking at me. I run and try not to think about anything. Just pound myself on. My lungs feel like they're about to collapse, poor abused organs of mine, God knows they're clogged enough already without having to work overtime. I don't have expensive running shoes either, the kind that are molded to your feet and equipped with special cushioning. Just my old sneakers, which are not aerodynamic, just ugly as shit and twice as uncomfortable. *(Pause. Annie laughs shortly, without amusement.)*

So I guess this isn't the kind of thing you guys are looking for, huh? *(She listens to the muffled reply.)* What's that? Whatever I care to talk about? Whatever. It's kind of strange, just sitting here and rambling about whatever comes into my head. *(Listens to comment.)* Therapeutic? Ridiculous! Because no matter how hard you scribble on those clipboards, you aren't going to crack into this! *(Gestures at herself violently:)* Really! Don't look at me like that, so calm, you've got to know it drives me crazy, and it's not fair. I'm not going anywhere and you damn well know it. Just because I told you about running doesn't mean anything. It doesn't mean anything! *(Struggles to gain control of her voice:)* Jesus, what a mess. *(Pause.)*

Well, I know what I want to talk about. Let me see. It was last summer . . . *(Lapses into silence.)*

Shits! Cunts! Mother-fucking perverts!

(Annie surveys the panel with a detached interest.)

I must say I'm impressed. Good facial control, y'all. Not even a twitch. You must get some real cases in here, huh? Not fazed by a few expletives, a dash of obscenity, you're well trained. Saint Joseph Reformatory must see some genuine cutups. Not like little old me, I bet I'm pretty mild compared to the freaks. The real freaks. The ones who eat their mothers. Do you get those? People who eat their mothers? *(Pause.)* I would never eat my mother. She's pickled from cheap Southern beer . . . and the breath of all the men she's kissed. And the disappointment of her entire stunted life, though she would probably not admit it to you. Her meat would taste like Budweiser and Slim-Fast and spoiled as aged fruit. C'mon. Give me a rating. Am I a four-star young disturbed person, or only a two? Spicy, or not so spicy? No? Closemouthed, hmm. Not even a clue. Poor sports. How the hell do you expect me to bond with you if you won't even give me my progress report? You probably know best, though, yes I'm sure you do. As I was saying, I think it was last summer, wasn't that what I said? Yeah. I had a boyfriend, then . . . Or almost a boyfriend.

SANS-CULOTTES IN THE PROMISED LAND

Kirsten Greenidge

Seriocomic
Charlotte, midtwenties

> *Charlotte is a teacher, one of whose pupils is Greta, age eight, whose*
> *parents are extremely well-off black professionals. Charlotte believes*
> *strongly in education, particularly about black heritage and culture.*
> *Greta has been skipping classes, so Charlotte comes to her house where*
> *she meets Lena, Greta's nanny, to whom she gives flash cards she has*
> *made for Greta to teach her about her African heritage.*

CHARLOTTE: Class just isn't the same without Greta. . . .

She really shouldn't skip.

She needs to know about her roots. She deserves to be proud. I made these myself.

I call them Heritage Holders. Each kid's going to get their own set because they all have stuff they should be working on. Like this kid I teach on Wednesdays — Austin Hill? He needs work on realizing how many stringed instruments originally came from parts of Africa. People like to associate Africa with only drums and that's unfair, that's a total misconception. There were stringed instruments all *over* ancient Africa. Not just drums. *What* do you think of *that?* . . .

And this is for hair.

(Produces a bottle.)

I made it myself. With plants. I'm very good with plants. Everything I used I grew myself. Go ahead and read the label. . . .

You can't buy better, not even from those fancy brands. I did research. About ancient African hair and I came up with this recipe, this fabulous, fabulous recipe. I can grow anything anywhere. Go ahead and read the label. . . .

This really is a nice house. You must get *paid*, girl, 'cause they got the bling-bling goin' *on*, OK?

(Charlotte takes a look around the room.) . . .

I'm talkin' Ba-*ank,* right? Right? . . .

(Charlotte takes a look around the room again.)

She *really* shouldn't skip. Cause I mean: them being the only people of "col-OR" up in this neighborhood — she *really* needs to know her roots. If I could rope in their parents they'd all be better off. But my adult classes never fill up. They think they can do Kwanzaa once a year, *maybe* even read some book about Juneteenth to stay in touch and it's a shame. Now use this twice a day and your hair will regain its natural strength in no time. Trust me. Read the label. . . .

You've got to treat yourself like the Nubian Princess you are. . . .

Cause they won't, let me tell you. I used to do the nanny thing. Couldn't handle it. Could not handle it. Especially with the colored folks, if you know what I mean. They think they're all that just cause they've got some change, right? . . .

Make sure she does those flash cards. She needs them.

SANS-CULOTTES IN THE PROMISED LAND
Kirsten Greenidge

Seriocomic
Charlotte, midtwenties

> *Charlotte is a teacher, one of whose pupils is Greta, age eight, whose*
> *parents are extremely well-off black professionals. Charlotte believes*
> *strongly in education, particularly about African heritage and cul-*
> *ture. Here, she is talking to Lena, the family's nanny, who we have*
> *learned is illiterate.*

CHARLOTTE: *Girrrrl.* This family is *wacked.* I mean they are *gone*, oh my
goodness. First I ring the bell for near to an hour before Broomhilda
(Mimics Carrmel.) answers the door and I'm like can I *please* talk to
Lena, thank you very much — that cousin I have? She's gonna hook
you up go-*od*. Literacy is legacy and all that so don't you worry but
first I have to finish my story, 'cause *then* when I get into the kitchen
the mother's like "Lena's *working,* you know" — *you know* — like we're
on some English moor, like she's some Parisian aristo-crat or some
such nonsense — I minored in French Studies, I know a thing or two
about those French rich people. Got their ass *whooped.* She wants to
play some role? OK by me as long as I get a role, too. I'll be a sans-
culotte, one of those French workers wanted to overthrow every-thang,
you know what I'm saying? Natural rights, natural state; none of this
abuse of wealth, of privilege, right? *Right?*
   (She looks at Lena.)
   Why're you on the floor like that? . . .
   Did you have an accident or something? . . .
   Why're you covered in their dirty clothes? . . .
   You *are*. . . .
   But we're goin' to free your mind, girl, me and my cousin got
to — *(The letters clang in the machine.)*

How are you supposed to get work done with a machine that clangs around like that? They probably blame you first chance if something shrinks, if something comes back a little worse for wear when it's not your fault. It's the machine. The system; *their system.* Ah-ha? You know?

SANS-CULOTTES IN THE PROMISED LAND
Kirsten Greenidge

Dramatic
Lena, twenty-five

Lena is a nanny who works for a well-off black family. She, too, is black. Here, she confesses to Charlotte, a teacher, that she is illiterate.

LENA: I used to want to be a stewardess. I know I'd look smart in that uniform. . . .

But there's tests. . . .

Letters get mixed up before I can make them fit together. . . .

The principal's son was my sweetheart; so I got my diploma: I wasn't one of those dropouts that smoke behind the Wal-Mart. . . .

I found my way. I'm not stupid. I pay attention. I had a teacher who was real into words, real into saying words the right way. I paid close attention to every little thing she said, and it worked: I don't sound like one of those people on the TV who can't put a sentence together, can't hardly talk: I'm not stupid. I keep up with everything. Even my bills. Each bill I get I send to my grandmother in Fort Worth. Over the phone she tells me how to make out my checks. The only problem right now is that washing machine. Greta's going to be walking around in rags if I don't tell them about me soon. People usually understand after I explain, after I tell them that letters don't work for me. Letters twist around before my head gets a chance to figure them out. People usually understand, but sometimes, sometimes they don't. That's . . . that's what happened at my last place. The mother there would write me things. I was really good at figuring them out except this one time, my last time, I wasn't, so good. It was a birthday party. I was supposed to take her two girls to this birthday party. She wrote the directions on this piece of paper. Easy, I thought. I just get the big one to read it, say my eyes hurt, or I forgot my glasses. I got a whole list of things I can say. And I can drive OK but directions, when they're on paper like that, are no good. So I stay calm. I drive around for a little. I wait. I drive a little more, then I make a joke: I say "Hey, make yourself useful." I give a little laugh, too, to go with the joke. But the big one, the ugly one with the big teeth she says "No." Just "No" flat out like that. She says it's not her job, it's mine. She says it's what her mother pays me good money for. So I ask the little one. I don't get huffy I just ask the little one if she can read. But. She can't. So I drive. Around and around 'til they both fall asleep. Big teeth and her sister. Useless. I drive thinking maybe I'll see a house with balloons. But I don't. Next day the agency calls. They say don't go to work today. They say I get one more chance before they have to let me go. This is my one more chance but they keep leaving me notes. I hate that. How am I supposed to keep my job if they write me notes?

SEVEN STAGES OF AN AFFAIR

Lorraine Forrest-Turner

Dramatic
Caroline, thirties to forties

> *Caroline is a married woman having an affair with a married man.*
> *In this direct address to the audience, she talks about her lover.*

CAROLINE: *(Slowly, enjoying every second of the memory.)* They get it all
wrong, you know, men. They think it has something to do with hair
and muscles and the size of their penises. But they're wrong. It's the
words, the talking, the looking into our face and searching our souls
that wins us over.

I loved his mind. I loved the way his mind explored my mind.
I loved his body and what it did to me. And what I did to it. I even
loved the fact that he was married, that he could have been doing
something else, with someone else, but he wasn't. He was with me.
He had deliberately given up his free time to be with me. He had
had a choice and he had picked me.

I couldn't remember when I had been so happy. *(Delighted with
herself.)* I became the perfect everything. I understood difficult clients,
insisted Helen take long lunches, played games with the girls, took
Beryl shopping, stopped nagging Robert, made the first move in our
marital bed and never once asked Tony about Linda. I don't know if
I was in love with Tony or just in love with the person I became when
I was with him. All that mattered was that I felt amazing and life just
couldn't get better.

SOCCER MOMS
Kathleen Clark

Dramatic
Nancy, midforties

> *This is an insightful play about three women who have become*
> *friends while they wait on the sidelines during their kids' soccer*
> *matches and practice. Nancy, one of the moms, is talking to another*
> *mom about how she has been thinking about her life.*

NANCY: You got it wrong, Lynn, nobody looks down on you. They're intimidated by you. *I'm* intimidated by you. But I . . . I *admire* you,
don't you know that? It's just . . . *(She sighs.)*

You know why you don't see any pictures?

(Nancy empties her camera bag upside down and rolls of undevel-
oped film fall on the ground.)

I never develop them. I say it's the kids' fault. That I don't have
time. I guess that's partially true, but . . . *(Pause.)*

You know what's killing me? I keep thinking I'm missing out on
something. I used to have this ecstasy about life that would make me
feel so alive, so joyful that I would just smile with it. And now . . .

Now I think about dying. In the past six months, there was both Mary
and my sister-in-law. Did you know that right here, on this bench,
Mary sat next to me one Sunday afternoon just a year ago. It was a
game that very few of us showed up for — she looked around, searching for people, and then she said, with such anger in her voice that
she was shaking, "Where is everybody? What could they be doing
that's so much more important than watching their children play?"
I was allowed for a few moments to look through the eyes of a woman
who was seeing life as clearly as you can see it — with a pure and
unobstructed vision. And her words hit me. Profoundly. Where *was*
everybody? She knew that with what time she had left all she wanted
to do was look at her children. . . .

And then, not more than a couple of months after that, my sister-in-law made that rare visit to our house. I told you about her — she had breast cancer. . . .

She said to me, how are you, and I started talking about the kids and she said, no, no, *you,* how are *you,* are you going back to work, are you really going to become a photographer, and before I could answer she begins to cry and says she wished she had worked at something that was just hers, that belonged to her. That she had actually written the book that she always talked about, but never took the time to do. She had two wonderful boys, but this is what she wanted to talk about. So, you see — children, work, there's always going to be some regret, so I keep thinking if I could just find out what mine will be, maybe I could do something about it. But I don't know how. The only thing I know for sure is my kids bring me joy, they mean everything in the world to me, so, see? What am I talking about? . . .

Whatever it is, I think if I don't do something soon, it's going to be too late.

SORCERESS
Don Nigro

Dramatic
Fay, thirty-seven

> *In the autumn of 1867, Fay has returned to the Pendragon house in east Ohio, after many years, to reclaim both the house and its master, John Pendragon, for her own. Years ago, as a servant in the house, she'd been sent away forcibly to Maryland by John's father, Zachary Pendragon, after he learned that John had impregnated Fay, who was actually Zach's illegitimate child, and thus John's sister. After the Civil War, Fay has appeared again to claim what she feels is her inheritance, and resumed her affair with her now married half-brother John. But Fay is not entirely in her right mind, and here she speaks to her sleeping daughter, Holly, about her very mixed but passionate feelings about the house and her tormented lover.*

FAY: Night in the dark house. Owls mourn. God makes truth like Sunday wine. Love is the best poison. I try to sleep but I hear voices in the woods. I dreamed I saw him in deep woods, sitting in a patch of ferns, a dark man, the evil one, my beloved, dark angel of my destruction. Yet I forgive him, massive old god with cracks in his soul. I will always love the way the sunlight strikes the earth here on an autumn morning. There is no escape when the Devil is your lover. Dead people in the pond. I see them standing at the end of the field, whispering in my brain. I love the woods, the myriad of small creatures living out their lives. They survive by devouring. He will come at night to touch me, or to kill me. I hear him in the woods like death. No one can kill you once you're dead. That's the great advantage of it. All he can think of is me, hunter of my soul. Winding paths through the woods. Twisted like naked lovers in the dark. Let the Devil in, you lose your soul. We made love in the pantry. He put honey on my nipples, licked me clean. We made love on the roof and nearly rolled off and died together. Near the edge is always best. In the grave-yard, crows landed on the tombstone beside us but we didn't stop. It was so cold. I thought I would die of pleasure, spidering through me like heat lightning, dead men's fingers clutching at my womb. He had me in the barn, under the wagon, against the wall of the linen closet, in the springhouse with the snakes. Then our father found us in the attic, and he went away and never answered one of my letters. The house remains inside me like a child.

STILL LIFE
From *Special Days*
Seth Kramer

Dramatic
Michelle, twenties to thirties

Michelle is in a hospital gown, her hands are wrapped.

MICHELLE: That what they all say. The fucking head shrinks who won't
leave me alone now. That's their line of crap.

(Vicious.) "Time to let the healing begin. Let's talk about what
you're feeling. What you're afraid of." I don't need to hear this shit
from you!

(Beat.)

A few times a week, you know, they come in here and prod me.
The doctors. The psychoanalysts. The physical therapists. And we go
through the same routine every time. They — they take needles and
poke at my hands. I watch them do this. Each finger, my palms, my
thumbs. Watching for any kind of reaction. "Did I feel that?" No.
"Can I move this?" No. "What sensation do you get when I do that?"
Nothing! They give me balls to squeeze, and "fine motor" tasks to
practice. They hook me up to a machine and take turns running elec-
trical currents through my stumps. Just to see which fingers twitch
a little and which ones remain lifeless.

(Beat.)

We have the talks. The talks about . . . About degrees of
progress . . . about long-term improvement and adaptive skills for
the real world and all that shit.

(Beat.)

That's my life now.

(Beat.)

You do a thing long enough, your whole life, I guess . . . I don't
really think it matters what that thing is . . . Bowling, playing poker,

art . . . I don't think it matters. Eventually it becomes you — that part of you that gives you a reason to wake up and breath every day. I mean, that's what it's all about, right?

(Beat.)

Your purpose, right?

(Pause.)

The FIRE took that from me. It took everything. Every single thing I ever made — Painted — All of it just torched to high hell. You have no idea what that means. What that felt like.

(Pause.)

I was meant to burn there, with everything else. You should have left me.

STONE COLD DEAD SERIOUS

Adam Rapp

Dramatic
Shaylee, seventeen

> *Shaylee, a teenaged runaway, is here talking to her younger brother,*
> *Wynne, who is a video game genius.*

SHAYLEE: Wynne, you know about six months ago I had a baby? It came
out dead. It was about the size of a tomato. I put it in a McDonald's
bag and threw it in the garbage. I talked about it in group today. How
I keep dreamin' about it. How sometimes it's huge and it's eatin' ham-
burgers at that Wendy's Oasis on 294. How I always wake up all
fucked up and cryin'.

This nun told me that God's tryin' to talk to me and that I should
use the opportunity to ask him for forgiveness. Like I should start
prayin' and shit.

In group we had to go around a circle and describe our own personal picture of God. The crack addict chick said God was Smokey
the Bear. I said he's like this old freak wrapped in a shower curtain
and he's got this big holy boner. And he's eatin' one of those side sal-
ads from Kentucky Fried Chicken.

Black was all, "Naw, man, God's a meat eater." His personal picture of God is this old buff ancient-lookin' fucker in a toga. And he's got
a perm and he's at the Sizzler eatin' a steak. Pretty funny, ain't it? . . .

Group's pretty cool. You get to talk about yourself, you know?
Listen to all these fucked-up stories. Some people just sit there. You
don't even gotta say nothin' if you don't wanna . . .

In the book there's this whole thing about God, but it ain't all
phony. The brother calls him the Fat Lady. It's actually pretty cool,
Wynne. They learn about stuff, you know? Like how to get through
the shitty times . . .

Ma's talkin' about you like you're her hero. She paid off the house yesterday. And Pop's seein' this back specialist in Mount Prospect. And I guess Marna's husband's gonna come over and look at the house to see about central air.

Pop's callin' you the Champ. They're on their way right now . . .

Dr. Kennedy said I can go home next month. I might do this halfway house thing first, but I'd get to crash at home on the weekends. Urine samples every three days. Try your luck, piss in a cup.

Ma says I've been approved to re-enroll at Norridge, too. If I catch up in school they're gonna let me back on the track team. Mr. Mecklo asked me to run the mile again but I was like, fuck that, I wanna polevault.

Fly over some shit, you know? . . .

I'm gonna stay clean this time, Wynne, I really am . . .

THE STORY
Tracey Scott Wilson

Dramatic
Jessica, thirties

> *Jessica's husband was murdered when the couple stopped for gaso-*
> *line in a black neighborhood. Here she is talking to a detective about*
> *the crime.*

JESSICA: I want to change my statement. It was a girl.

> *(Pause.)*

It was a girl. . . .

> *(Pause.)*

Now, I hear they're wondering if maybe it was a student of Tim's seeking revenge or something. Did you hear that? . . .

But you know black kids don't really do that, do they? Black kids don't go into the cafeteria and shoot up everybody or stalk teachers and shoot them. Isn't that true? If one of Tim's black students was angry with him, the black student would have shot Tim right there in the moment. Isn't that right?

> *(Pause.)*

Isn't that right?

> *(Detective doesn't answer.)*

Then we wouldn't be here. The black student would have been arrested and we wouldn't be here.

> *(Pause.)*

A couple of weeks ago some people were even saying I had something to do with it. Like it was all some elaborate scheme I thought up.

> *(Pause.)*

I don't know if it was a girl dressed like a guy or a guy dressed like a girl dressed like a guy. I only know the killer was black. *(Pause.)* The killer was black.

THE STORY
Tracey Scott Wilson

Dramatic
Latisha, a black teenager

> *Latisha is a street-tough black girl who has told many stories to*
> *Yvonne, an aggressive black journalist, about the all-girl gang she's*
> *in, which Yvonne has used as a basis for stories she's written for her*
> *newspaper. Here, Latisha confesses that these stories were all fantasy.*

LATISHA: I'm not . . . I'm not in a gang. *(Pause.)* And I don't know about
any murder. . . .

I was just playing with you. I was just playing. . . .

You know I just . . . I go to boarding school and they are fascinated by a ghetto girl like me. Fascinated. How do you get your hair
like that? Have you ever seen anybody murdered? I get so sick of it.
So, you know, I just make up shit to pass the time. I tell them I'm
in a gang, and my mother is on crack. They think I'm supposed to
be like that so I just . . . My mother is a librarian. I barely leave the
house when I come home from school.

(Seeing Yvonne's expression.)

Are you . . . Are you alright? . . .

You helped me? No . . . I . . . See . . . I . . . *(Pause.)* Listen, I'm
sorry. I'm . . . *Sono molto spiacente. (Pause.)* I tell you it's hard keep-
ing it real sometimes. *(Pause.)* I don't know . . . *(Pause.)* When I saw
you that day I wondered if it would work on one of us. I mean, I
could tell you were different. Not really one of us. Like me kinda.
Just the way you . . . I don't know. *(Pause.)* I look around my neighborhood and I wish I could move. Everybody acts so stupid. But
they're not stupid. They just act stupid. You know Franz Fanon says
the oppressed are taught to believe the worst about themselves. So I
just wanted to see. I spoke Italian and German to you and you still

believed I was in a gang. *(Pause.)* Just like the people at school. *(Pause.)* Just like them. *(Pause.)* . . .

There are no AOB's. There are no AOB's. I'm calling the paper and telling the truth.

SUGARBABY
Frank Cwiklik

Dramatic
Sugarbaby, seventeen

> *Bailey Sugarman —aka Sugarbaby, seventeen years old, a bright,*
> *vivacious young girl, in love with America, Americana, and life —*
> *stands before the Lincoln Memorial on the Mall in Washington,*
> *D.C., before a crowd of thousands. She's become a media celebrity,*
> *having just run away from home with her best friend, Jesus — a*
> *mechanic who thinks he's Elvis, to see America. Trouble is, some folks*
> *think she's been kidnapped by Muslim terrorists. Other folks think*
> *she's run away to make a political statement on capitalism and*
> *democracy. Others think she's a new folk hero, a riposte to the plas-*
> *tic, biased media. But others — including conservative talk show*
> *host Rod Butane and liberal documentarian Mitch Common — just*
> *see her as one more shot at glory, a money-making media flash point.*
> *And they're here, too, hogging the glory, starting a riot, stoking the*
> *anger and resentment of this increasingly polarized and divided na-*
> *tion . . . until, like an avenging angel, Sug appears to set everything*
> *right . . .*

SUGARBABY: I ran away from home. I was not kidnapped. I was not the
victim of Muslim terrorists. I was not brainwashed. I am not making a political statement. I am not trying to sell you anything. I just
wanted to see America. And I did.

And she's sick.

Sick in her heart, and in her soul, and I don't know that we'll
ever be able to make her right again. But you don't give up on someone you love. And you don't cure someone who's sick by yelling at
them, and hating them, and mistrusting them, and abusing them,
and forgetting all the reasons you loved them in the first place! . . .

(To Mitch.) I'm talking about you, asshole! You don't get it, do

you? This fight isn't about you! This country is not here as your personal experiment, to argue about, and fight over, and use as a bully pulpit! And how dare you assume that because you got some kind of damn college degree that you know anything, anything at all about me, or anybody! Even when you say something people can agree with, they wanna disagree just because you're all so ass-lipped and nasty, that you turn people off without even trying! You are smug, self-centered, and mean, and you're a pollutant. . . .

(To Rod.) And you, you egotistical, moralistic, smug, arrogant sunuvabitch! . . .

It's all America number one with you, isn't it, if it's white, it's right, everything's about God, mother, and apple pie! Well, there is no God, some people aren't fit to be mothers — . . .

And I never did like apple pie anyway, and ya'll are living thirty years in the past, refusing to believe that anyone could disagree with you, live their own life their own way, and still be very, very happy! Anytime anyone disagrees with you, it couldn't possibly be because you're wrong, it must mean they're un-American! Bullshit! You're right, America is the most important word, but you don't even know what that means! It means that God is whatever we want it to be, and America is whatever we can make of her, and hope isn't your personal Goddamn possession to be doled out like fucking war rations, you selfish sunsabitches!!!

TEN UNKNOWNS
Jon Robin Baitz

Dramatic
Julia, mid-to-late twenties

> *Julia is a biology grad student who has come to Mexico to gather data for her thesis project about the worldwide disappearance of frogs. There, she has been befriended by a famous American painter named Raphelson, to whom she tells this story.*

JULIA: *(Quietly, weary, fierce.)* You have no idea what I am. And I am many things, but a child isn't one of them. *(She says nothing for a moment.)* . . .

But — You turn me into one, don't you? I was married when I was eighteen. It's like waking up with a tattoo. You think "How did this happen?" And you know who he was? He was basically Judd. He had illustrated an article I was writing on "concentric circles of responsibility," little pencil scratchings — he got it, all the ramifications — and it ate him alive — he saw it so clearly — in the atavistic muck and the sand, and all the inhabitants of a one-foot tidal pool at Point Reyes, he saw what we had become. He was not from this planet at all. Fury, shooting up, binges, first as a joke, and then seriously. Anyway, I'm not a child. . . .

(Flat.) He threw himself off the roof of a hotel in the Tenderloin. *(Beat. Raphe does not know what to do.)* We were nineteen. Cut his wrists first. That hadn't worked, so then he jumped while I was out looking for him all night. . . .

(Shaking her head, bitter.) In and out of facilities. One week clean, then not. Tried to save himself through work on a children's book, but he never could get it down, and I tried and tried and got angrier and more tired, and he got more and more guilty and humiliated. Then one night he's dead outside a Pakistani restaurant we liked for the goat, and I'm pregnant. I go to my parents for help. No idea what

89

to do. My dad, they'd been at Berkeley, they'd both been in S.D.S., now they're both corporate lawyers — suggested, "Well, have an abortion: We're pro-choice." My mom suggests, "Put it up for adoption." No one — no one — suggested I perhaps keep this baby or really even offered to help.

I opted for the abortion. I regret it every day, because I want a kid. I went in. And I thought I would feel something. Anything — feel regret or freedom or release or rage. But I went to the clinic in Oakland, and came home, and I felt nothing. I felt numb. One of the walking dead of my time. Watched TV for two years straight. Seventies sitcoms. I finally fit in perfectly. Finally I was like everyone else. Nothing much mattered. '82, '83, '87 . . . I had gone dead like the place I lived in. *(She smiles at him.)* You want to know why I was so . . . happy to come here and live with you? Because you were born before this ice-age hit, and you never gave up. My husband did. But under the wreckage and the disaffection and the rage, he was a gentle soul. I know that voice, and I love it.

À TROIS
Barry Hall

Dramatic
B, a woman in her twenties to thirties

B is a working girl, here talking to a potential "client."

B: *(To audience — perhaps to one audience member.)* What can I say? What
do you want me to say? It beats working? The money's good? Yeah,
sometimes. Better than nine to five. And the *people* you meet! I'm
not saying you'll meet the president of the United States — though
I wouldn't rule it out — but — well, just the other night, do you
know who I met at this very bar? I met a client — "client" — from
Bismarck who was the *biggest* seller of industrial drill bits in the *whole*
of southwestern North Dakota.

Beats working.

Oh, and this guy — this client — (that's another thing — the *stories* you hear) — told me all about his experience in the war (the Gulf
War, remember that one?) — "just like playing a video game" — and
how he came back and married his childhood sweetheart and fought
to survive in the untamed southwestern North Dakota industrial drill-
bit jungle, which eventually brought him . . . to me. Business. Travel.
They get lonely.

I have a master's in philosophy. Well, I'm really just a semester
short. But I usually leave that part out. Makes for a better story.

I did some acting in college. Ms. Kinghorn, my — business man-
ager, says "the theater is the best school for" our — profession. I had
the lead in one show — *Our Town*. Well, not *Our Town*, actually,
but — makes for a better story.

Acting. That's it, basically. That's all there is to it. You play the
role. Whatever that may be. Whatever may be — *required.* Shy. Del-
icate. Brazen. Dominant. Vulnerable. Aggressive. Demure. Mysterious. Honest.

I *have* been honest with you, haven't I? Isn't that what you wanted?

You know, I have a bottle of wine in my room. We could speak so much more — *freely* there.

Oh, of course. Of *course*. Just leave everything up to me. Don't worry about a thing. Room 326. I'll leave the door unlocked.

VALHALLA
Paul Rudnick

Comic
Sally, a young woman in her early twenties, Texan

Sally is engaged to be married, but she has strong feelings for another man, her groom-to-be's best friend, who's been doing time in prison.

SALLY: Some people think that I had — feelings for James Avery, but that is just not true. But before he — went away, he always used to say something which I will never forget. He would say that he'd been studying the situation since kindergarten, and that he'd made lists and charts and held a personal pageant, and that he had finally determined that I was the prettiest girl in all of Dainesville. And he said that the prettiest girl can give people hope, and brighten their day, and wasn't that just a wonderful thing to say? Especially for a delinquent? And ever since then, whenever I look in the mirror, I see Eleanor Roosevelt. Only, of course, pretty. I mean, Mrs. Roosevelt works so hard, trying to help the poor and the downtrodden, but can you imagine how much more she could do, if she were pretty? And of course, there's also inner beauty, but inner beauty is tricky, because you can't prove it. I've thought a lot about this, you know, about beauty and goodness, and all the different religions? I mean, Buddha is chubby — face it. And Confucius was all old and scraggly and, I imagine, single. And you're not even allowed to have a picture of Mohammed — was it the teeth? I don't know. But Jesus is always really pretty, with perfect skin and shiny hair, it's like God was saying, look to Jesus, for tips. But I know there's that German man, Adolf Hitler, and he thinks that everyone should be perfect and blue-eyed and beautiful, but that's wrong too, because then who would be the best friends? And I don't want to be vain or prideful, so I always remember what James said, in one of his letters. He said that there are only two things which really matter in life: youth and beauty.

VALHALLA
Paul Rudnick

Comic
Natalie Kippelbaum, forties to fifties

> *Natalie Kippelbaum is a modern-day tour guide, a peppy Ameri-*
> *can woman from Long Island. She wears a gold lamé jogging suit,*
> *accessorized with a large button which says "GUIDE," a leopard*
> *skin fannypack, a major highlighted hairdo, plenty of jewelry, over-*
> *size eyeglasses and hot-pink-and-silver-lamé sneakers. Natalie is a*
> *born entertainer and hostess, thrilled to share her enthusiasm for*
> *Ludwig and his castles. She is played by the same actress who plays*
> *the Queen. Natalie speaks to the audience, and her unseen tour*
> *group.*

NATALIE: Hi! I'm Natalie Kippelbaum, and welcome to Temple Beth
Shalom's Whirlwind European Adventure Castles of Bavaria Plus
Wine Tasting and Wienerschnitzel Potpourri Tour. Yes. The bus will
be here any second, so let's get started. And I know what you're thinking, you're going, Natalie, from Long Island, what are you doing with
Ludwig? Well, three years ago, I hit bottom. First, my husband, he
dies, from lung cancer. Fun. But then, my daughter, she loses her
job. Then my son, Debbie — enough said. And I'm in my Hyundai,
and I'm about to drive off a bridge, like in a Hyundai that's even
necessary, and then — I hear music. Gorgeous, operatic music. You
know — NPR. And I think, where is that music coming from, I
mean, where was it born? So I get on a plane, and I'm here. And the
minute I step into that grotto — I'm happy. I'm high. And today
we're going to see something even more beautiful, because in 1883,
Ludwig decided to build his copy of Versailles. *(She pronounces the*
word with a thick Long Island accent — "Versoy.") That's right —
Versailles.

VALHALLA
Paul Rudnick

Comic
Natalie Kippelbaum, forties to fifties

> *Natalie Kippelbaum is a modern-day tour guide, a peppy Ameri-*
> *can woman from Long Island. She wears a gold lamé jogging suit,*
> *accessorized with a large button which says "GUIDE," a leopard*
> *skin fannypack, a major highlighted hairdo, plenty of jewelry, over-*
> *size eyeglasses and hot-pink-and-silver-lamé sneakers. Natalie is a*
> *born entertainer and hostess, thrilled to share her enthusiasm for*
> *Ludwig and his castles. She is played by the same actress who plays*
> *the Queen. Natalie speaks to the audience, and her unseen tour*
> *group.*

NATALIE: Ludwig couldn't stop building — he was hooked, like on crack.
He would race from one construction site to the next, at midnight,
in a sleigh drawn by six white stallions — goyim! He did a Moor-
ish pavilion, a medieval hunting lodge, and a theater at Bayreuth,
with perfect acoustics, where the works of Richard Wagner are still
performed to this day. And I know, that Wagner, he was no friend
of the Jews. So you know what I call him?

(She uses the soft, American "W.")

Wagner. Dickie Wagner. Ha! He'd die!

What's that, Mrs. Slatkin? So what happened to Ludwig? You'll
see in just a minute, when we make our final stop. But just remember,
if you can't give up everything, even your life itself, for what you truly
believe in, well, then why bother?

So whenever I'm down, whenever I think about terrorists and
starving children and Debbie trying to find shoes — I think of Ludwig. So grab your bottled water and your Instamatics, and look out
your window, on the left, because here it comes, all the way up on
that mountaintop, it's Ludwig's ultimate dream, his home of the gods,

his swan song, I'm kvelling, wait till you see it, if it were a person, I'd have sex with it, and I'm not a young woman. There it is — excuse me, I need a moment.

(She takes a deep breath, composing herself, overcome.)

There it is — Valhalla!

WHOSE FAMILY VALUES!
Richard Abrons

Dramatic
Doreen, twenties, black

> *Doreen is dating a white man whose family doesn't know about her,*
> *and to whom she is talking. Actually, she is telling off her boyfriend's*
> *father.*

DOREEN: What has my experience got to do with it? What if I never gave
a thought to the child I killed? Am I so important that laws should
be made based on *my* experience? . . .

But let me tell you something, Mr. Boyd. You can devote your
life to fetuses, but I'm devoting mine to children — children who
are bounced around foster homes, children who drop out of school,
children who are homeless, children who take drugs, children who
have health problems no one gives a damn about, and yes Mr. Boyd,
children who have no business having children. Unwanted children
who are abused — small children who are burned or beaten so badly
they have to go to the hospital. You can see that time and time again,
and it never fails to tear your heart out. Get those unwanted fetuses
out, get them out as babies and we'll have a never-ending supply of
children to rescue except there aren't enough of us and there isn't the
money for it. Yes, I killed my child. It was so very hard, but I wasn't
ready for her. And she wasn't a child; she was a mass of cells. But in
my mind she was my child so it wasn't easy. Well, do you think it's
easy to take care of an eleven-year-old boy, Timmy Sandini, who has
tried to commit suicide three times because no one but me cares
whether he lives or dies? Oh, Mr. Boyd, these things are a hell of a
lot more complex than quoting a chapter in the Bible. It would be
good if you were not so sure of yourself. . . .

(Getting into it.) If you were not so sure that *you* were right and
the law was wrong, you would have called the police. And that is what
you should have done.

WOMEN ON FIRE
Irene O'Garden

Dramatic
Jordy, very elderly, but spry

> Women on Fire *is a series of monologues performed in New York by a single actress, Judith Ivey. All are direct addresses to audience.*

JORDY: Did you know you can fill a room with your joy? Did you know this is what people really want? Movement is the first commandment. You owe it to your body to obey it. Dancin' is the hymnal:

Fingers flinging alleluias. Torso-folding lamentation. Fierce, dance fierce, then light, like a swimmer skimming water. I might could tell you things more mysterious: How one body tells another it is beautiful. How the grace of flesh, physicality, the power of creation drip like spangles from your moving arm. And how you cannot hold to ecstasy, for ecstasy will crowd you out upon itself. These things I can tell you as certainly as worship, but I cannot tell you them in words.

Did you know it don't matter what happened when you was a child? You cannot hold to grievance for grievance will crowd you out upon itself. It will ice your body up, stop up your sap, truss up yourself like a old turkey. Where is them spangles now?

You got something to say, you stomp your history out across a floor. Pound on Mama Earth. She glad to hear from you. She can take it all. And your own limbs can answer any question put to them.

You wanna blame someone? Blame yourself for forgetting what's going on right now. The beauty of *this* world.

And don't tell me I don't know what grief is. I dance my drunk daddy. I dance my dead daughter.

Free ain't somethin' you get when you buy somethin'. It's a psalm you sing yourself.

Remember you can fill a room with your joy. Remember this is what *you* really want.

WOMEN ON FIRE
Irene O'Garden

Dramatic
Zatz, could be any age twenties to fifties

> Women on Fire *is a series of monologues performed in New York by a single actress, Judith Ivey. All are direct addresses to audience.*

ZATZ: *(Perched precariously with a spray can.)* Attention Shoppers! Is there a publisher in the house? Anywhere in this mega-ultra super-cyclopedic bookatorium? I'll get down off this bookcase when you bring me a publisher. And I'll spray-paint a book a minute until you do! Stand back! It's pointed at *Moby Dick* and I'm gonna use it! *(Pssss.)* Bye-bye Ahab! Took your whole life to nail him, and I got him in two seconds. Melville to Hellville.

Don't try to pull a ladder up! I'll spray you fast as you can climb. You don't know what else I got on me. No, dickhead, I'm not using. Words are all I use, man. I roll 'em into sentences and smoke 'em, one after the other, shooting right out of my fingers sometimes. Sometimes tips of orange fire swell and glow and pull me forward. Or blue smoky thoughts which where are they leading me? How can I capture them? Sometimes I stub them out before they're halfway done. Words are so mysterious, man. And they're free! Use all you want, there's always more. A day without words is like . . . Zatz my point. And Zatz my name. Z-A-T-Z. Because the purpose of a writer is to point things out. *Zatz* it. Zatz me. And you will not forget me. Sinclair Lewis. To the sewers! No one reads you any more anyway. *(Pssss.)*

Rights and Permissions

emphasis is laid upon the question of readings, permission for which must be secured from the author's agent in writing. The stage performance rights in *The Coming World* (other than first-class rights) are controlled exclusively by Dramatists Play Service, Inc., 440 Park Avenue South, New York, NY 10016. No professional or nonprofessional performance of the play (excluding the first-class professional performance) may be given without obtaining in advance the written permission of Dramatists Play Service, Inc., and paying the requisite fee. Inquiries concerning all other rights should be addressed to The Gersh Agency, 41 Madison Avenue, 33rd floor, New York, NY 10010. Attn: John Buzzetti.

THE DEATH OF FRANK. ©2000 by Stephen Belber. Reprinted by permission of John Buzzetti, The Gersh Agency, 41 Madison Avenue, 33rd floor, New York, NY 10010. CAUTION: Professionals and amateurs are hereby warned that *The Death of Frank* is subject to a royalty. It is fully protected under the copyright laws of the United States of America, and of all countries covered by the International Copyright Union (including the Dominion of Canada and the rest of the British Commonwealth), and of all countries covered by the Pan-American Copyright Convention and the Universal Copyright Convention, and of all countries with which the United States has reciprocal copyright relations. All rights, including professional, amateur, motion picture, recitation, lecturing, public reading, radio broadcasting, television, video or sound taping, all other forms of mechanical or electronic reproduction, such as information storage and retrieval systems and photocopying, and the rights of translation into foreign languages, are strictly reserved. Particular emphasis is laid upon the question of readings, permission for which must be secured from the author's agent in writing. The stage performance rights in *The Death of Frank* (other than first-class rights) are controlled exclusively by Dramatists Play Service, Inc., 440 Park Avenue South, New York, NY 10016. No professional or nonprofessional performance of the play (excluding the first-class professional performance) may be given without obtaining in advance the written permission of Dramatists Play Service, Inc., and paying the requisite fee. Inquiries concerning all other rights should be addressed to The Gersh Agency, 41 Madison Avenue, 33rd floor, New York, NY 10010. Attn: John Buzzetti.

DEBT. ©2003 by Seth Kramer. Reprinted by permission of Playscripts, Inc., from which the entire text is available in an acting edition, and which handles performance rights. Their addresses: Box 237060, New York, NY 10023. www.playscripts.com (Web site) Playscripts.com (Web site) 866-NEWPLAY (phone)

FEED THE HOLE. ©2003 by Michael Stock. The entire text has been published by New York Theatre Experience in *Plays and Playwrights 2004*. Address: Box 744, New York, NY 10274-0744. www.nytheatre.com. E-mail: info@newyorktheatreexperience.org

FIGHTING WORDS. ©2003 by Sunil Kuruvilla. Reprinted by permission of the author and the Joyce Ketay Agency, 630 9th Ave. #706, New York, NY 10036. The entire text of the play has been published in an acting edition by Dramatic Publishing Co., which also handles performance rights. Their address: Box 129, Woodstock, IL 60098

FIVE FLIGHTS. ©2004 by Adam Bock. Reprinted by permission of the William Morris Agency, Inc., 1325 Ave. of the Americas, New York, NY 10019. Their addresses: Box 237060, New York, NY 10023. www.playscripts.com (Web site) Playscripts.com (Web site) 866-NEWPLAY (phone)

FISHER KING. ©2004 by Don Nigro. Reprinted by permission of Samuel French, Inc., 45 W. 25th St., New York, NY 10010, which has published the entire text in an acting edition and which handles performance rights.

GOING TO ST. IVES. ©2003 by Lee Blessing. Reprinted by permission of Judy Boals, Judy Boals, Inc., 208 W. 30th St. #401, New York, NY 10001. The entire text has been published by Dramatists Play Service, 440 Park Ave. S., New York, NY 10016, which also handles performance rights.

102

3 1531 00276 8122